Becoming a Higher Level Teaching Assistant: Primary English

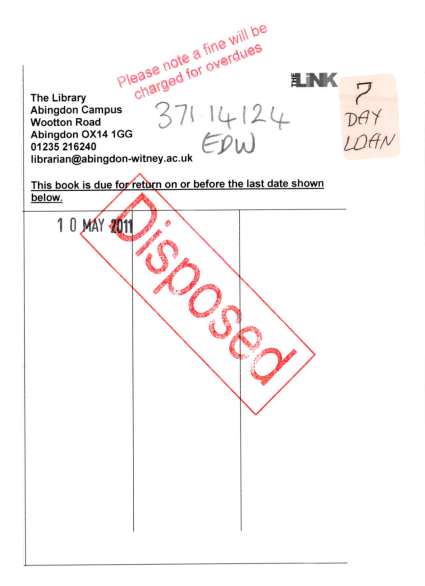

The Professional Teaching Assistant

Becoming a Higher Level Teaching Assistant: Primary English

● **Jean Edwards**

Learning Matters

12.00

First published in 2006 by Learning Matters Ltd.

British Library Cataloguing in Publication Data
A CIP record for this book is available from the British Library.

ISBN 13: 978 1 84445 046 5
ISBN 10: 1 84445 046 5

Project Management by Deer Park Productions
Cover design by Code 5 Design Associates Ltd
Typeset by Pantek Arts Ltd, Maidstone, Kent
Printed and bound in Great Britain by Bell & Bain Ltd, Glasgow

Learning Matters Ltd
33 Southernhay East
EXETER EX1 1NX
Tel: 01392 215560
info@learningmatters.co.uk
www.learningmatters.co.uk

Contents

The author

Jean Edwards is a Senior Lecturer in English Education at the University of Northampton. She has previously held posts as teacher and deputy head teacher at schools in Northamptonshire and as a head teacher at Priory Lower School in Bedford. She has been involved in curriculum development and the training of teachers and teaching assistants at local and national level. She is currently a trainer and assessor for HLTA at the University of Northampton.

Acknowledgements

The author is indebted to colleagues within the School of Education at the University of Northampton whose work and ideas have informed this book. I am also grateful to the many teaching assistants who have participated on courses provided through the School of Education and to their schools for the support which they have provided for both the students and myself.

Dedication

This book is dedicated to the teachers and teaching assistants I have worked with during my career. In particular to the staff at Priory Lower, whose commitment to the education of all children was an inspiration.

Introduction

HOW TO USE THIS BOOK

This book, along with the others in the Professional Teaching Assistant series, has been designed not only to assist you in achieving HLTA status, but also to encourage you to reflect upon and learn about the requirements of working in today's classrooms. This book is written in recognition of the fact that the important role played by teaching assistants (TAs) in our schools and colleges is finally being acknowledged, and that increasing numbers of TAs are seeking further training, qualifications and status within their schools.

This book has the primary objective of supporting TAs whose work is mainly focused upon learning and teaching in literacy and English with individuals, groups and the whole class. In addition to this it can support TAs who support and teach across the curriculum in primary schools, since the development and application of skills in English and literacy are integral to all learning and teaching experiences for younger children.

This book begins with the premise that its readers have made a commitment to achieving the highest standards in providing classroom support for all pupils. It sets out not only to assist the reader in gaining the standards for HLTA, but also provides opportunities for reflection upon how pupils learn and how they may best be supported in that process.

Each chapter introduces an area or aspect of the English curriculum. While a book of this nature can do little more than raise awareness of each of these areas, through a series of practical tasks and case studies it endeavours to assist the reader in contemplating and analysing those factors which may influence the success or failure of learners in a typical classroom in aspects of English and literacy.

It is anticipated that those who read this book are likely to have embarked upon a pathway, which they hope will lead them to gaining HLTA status. With this in mind, the book has been written to a set format which aims to assist the reader in gaining some understanding of issues, encourages them to consider these in respect of specific examples and to undertake a series of tasks to develop their own thinking and subject knowledge in respect of these issues.

Each chapter has a brief introduction, which is followed by an outline of the HLTA Standards to be considered within the chapter. Inevitably, some of the standards will be addressed in more than one chapter, while others are more tightly focused and may only be considered at a specific point in the book. Early in each chapter you will find a box which outlines what you should have learned once you have read the chapter and completed the tasks within it.

Chapter 2 introduces you to the range of documents that are used in schools to form the basis of literacy and English planning and teaching. Identifying and acquiring some of these documents will underpin activities in subsequent chapters. It also considers some issues related to planning at individual, group and whole-class levels. Chapters 3 to 5 cover the main areas of English – speaking and listening, reading and writing. Chapters 6 to 9 cover specific aspects of English such as phonics, grammar, punctuation and handwriting. These are aspects that require further more detailed consideration, but should also be related back to speaking and listening, reading and writing. Chapter 10 outlines issues in relation to assessment in literacy and English.

The case studies have all been drawn from the school experiences of colleagues and students with whom I have worked over the years. They are presented as a means of illustrating principles discussed in the chapter. You may consider these in respect of your own experiences and should always try to reflect upon them in a way that enables you to think about how you would deal with similar situations in your own school.

The practical tasks provided are designed to encourage you to gather evidence of your own, or your school's response to a range of situations related to the HLTA Standards. Some of the practical tasks encourage you to evaluate your own subject knowledge. You may use these self-audits as a platform from which to extend your subject knowledge where appropriate. In some instances you may choose to use the evidence gathered from undertaking these tasks as a contribution towards the assessment process. For some of the tasks you will need the co-operation of colleagues or others within your school. It is hoped that by participating in these tasks you may be enabled to engage in a professional dialogue which informs your own thinking and possibly that of others.

Both the case studies and the practical tasks encourage you to focus on specific aspects of literacy and English and the use of English and literacy knowledge, skills and understanding across the curriculum and in meaningful contexts. Some of them encourage you to consider your role in working in partnership with parents.

At the end of each chapter you will find a summary of key points which indicate some of the most important principles discussed and which you may wish to consider in respect of your own practice and that of others within your school.

This book does draw upon research and refers to a number of other key texts, but does so without wishing to overburden the reader with the task of needing to hunt for additional information unless they should choose so to do. Many of the resources referred to in this book are available on the DfES website and are likely to be present in your school. I have made reference to these because it is likely you can gain easy access to these through your school or acquire copies of your own. The references are listed at the end of each chapter and provide an indication of further reading which you may wish to pursue as you continue your path towards attaining HLTA status.

1. Meeting the Standards for the Higher Level Teaching Assistant

This book has been written with the aim of helping you to prepare for the new status of the Higher Level Teaching Assistant (HLTA) with a focus on the curriculum area of English. It may be that you are developing English as a specialist area in your HLTA assessment or perhaps you aim to improve your competence and confidence in this area of the curriculum.

In the publication *Time for Standards* (DfES 2002), the government set out its plans for the reform of the school workforce. This reform recognised that support staff can, and do, make an increasingly critical contribution to all aspects of the successful operation of schools. At the same time there was an important acknowledgement that with training and support many TAs can operate at a higher level than may have been recognised in the past.

The HLTA Standards were published in September 2003 (TTA 2004), and identified those skills and the understanding you will need to demonstrate in order to be awarded the status of HLTA. Many TAs when they first look at these standards suggest that they already meet many, if not all of them. You will find when we look at the standards in detail that this is often the case but that some standards may be more problematic to demonstrate than others. This may because of the specific situation in which you have been working, or related to a lack of training in respect of certain elements of the standards. However, the key point to understand is that the status of HLTA is awarded by the Teacher Development and Training Agency for Schools (TDA, formerly the Teacher Training Agency (TTA)) via a number of Approved Training Providers and that you will need to provide evidence to them that you can meet all of the standards as detailed. The main focus of this chapter is to help you to become familiar with the standards and to help you prepare for this assessment. Not every standard is applicable to the curriculum area of English but many are, and reference is made to these throughout the book.

Assessment of HLTA status

There are a number of underlying principles which inform the assessment of HLTA, and these can be identified under the following headings:

- School support for the candidate.
- Proficiency in literacy and numeracy (see Standard 2.6).
- Assessment must be manageable, rigorous and fit for purpose.
- Assessment must take no more time than is necessary to demonstrate competence.
- Assessment should be based on work that occurs during the normal course of duties.
- It is the responsibility of the candidate to record evidence in support of the assessment.

The first of these principles is important for anyone contemplating going forward for assessment. The support of the school is essential if you are to be able to gather all of the evidence which you require in order to demonstrate that you meet the required standards. Your head teacher will have to agree to your application to go on the HLTA route. It is also helpful to discuss this procedure with your immediate working colleagues who you will be asking to support you at various stages of the process. It is equally essential that you have a literacy or numeracy qualification at NVQ level 2 or its equivalent, as you will not be able to proceed successfully without this crucial evidence. Details of what constitutes these levels are available from the TDA website **www.tda.gov.uk**. The aim of the HLTA programme is that the assessment process should be linked to your normal workload; in other words, you should be in a position to use evidence from your daily working practice in order to support the assessment process. This aim, while laudable, has not, in most cases, been realised and the majority of candidates have undertaken a large amount of additional work in order to ensure that they gain sufficient evidence to satisfy the assessors.

Routes to achieving HLTA Status

There are three routes to achieving HLTA status. These are:

1. Assessment-only route. This is a three-day route spread over a term and is for more experienced TAs who feel that they already meet the standards.
2. Training route. This provides face-to-face training. The length and nature of this training are based upon a needs analysis. Candidates will opt into the training sessions they require. This route is for TAs who need training in certain standards before they apply for HLTA status.
3. Specialist HLTA routes for candidates working within just one curriculum area in a secondary school.

An early priority must be for you to decide which is the best route for you. This depends on your current level of expertise and training and your personal confidence in relation to the HLTA Standards. This is where having the support of colleagues in school may be particularly helpful in providing you with an opportunity to discuss how both you and they feel about your current experience and expertise. If you have limited experience of working in schools as a TA and have undertaken very limited training, you need to explore how you can extend your knowledge and experience and then apply to go on a HLTA route in the future. If you feel that you need further training in order to meet the standards, for example in the areas of special educational needs (SEN) or information and communications technology (ICT), then the full training route is likely to be the most appropriate for you. As mentioned above, this is based on a needs analysis and you will select the relevant training sessions. This training will be provided through face-to-face training and computer-based e-learning.

If you feel that you have considerable knowledge, experience and skills related to the HLTA Standards you should apply to go on the assessment-only route.

However, we would advise that before making this decision, you examine the HLTA Standards carefully in order to ensure that you are familiar with these, and will be able to provide clear evidence of your ability to meet them in assessment. The task at the end of this chapter is designed to enable you to do this. The specialist HLTA route is aimed at TAs working in secondary schools, particularly where they are supporting within a single curriculum area. At the time of writing, this route is in the early stages of development.

Another possible route to HLTA is for those students who are taking a foundation degree or similar degree course. The increase in opportunities to undertake foundation degrees has, in many instances, been welcomed by TAs as enabling them to further their own professional knowledge and skills. You will still need to apply for a place on the HLTA via your local education authority (LEA) and undertake the assessment-only route.

There are a number of stages for you to go through and some TAs reading this book will already be on a HLTA programme, while others are considering applying. The six stages for the three-day assessment route are:

● Candidate information
● Two-day briefing
● Assessment tasks
● One day briefing and review
● School visit
● Decision communicated.

PRACTICAL TASK

Consider the position of the following TAs who are considering being assessed for the HLTA. Which of the three assessment routes would you recommend to them and why?

Susan is a TA currently working within the Foundation Stage. She currently working towards a Foundation Degree for Teaching Assistants and hopes to achieve Qualified Teacher Status after she is awarded an honours degree. There are two Reception classes in the Foundation Stage in her school and Susan plans and delivers sessions on numeracy and creative developments. Susan works closely with the Reception teacher. Susan wants to achieve HLTA status as a way of getting onto an employment-based route into teaching.

John is a TA who has worked in the school for one year and has an excellent awareness of autism spectrum disorders. He works with a Year 5 pupil who has a diagnosis of autistic spectrum disorder and now would like to expand his opportunities to work across the school with other groups of pupils.

Angela has undertaken a number of courses for TAs at her local university and worked as a Specialist Teaching Assistant for 6 years. She works with individual pupils, groups and a whole class for dance. She has experience of teaching dance to children and adults at her local community centre.

It is possible to suggest that in the examples provided, John should do the full training route, Angela an assessment course and Susan needs to opt for the assessment-only route as she is undertaking a foundation degree. However, much will depend upon the individual circumstances of the interested TAs as well as factors such as the support of the school in providing opportunities for gaining experience and the confidence with which they each approach the task. These are important factors which you need to consider in committing yourself to this process. Whichever route is most relevant to you, you will have to undertake the same assessment procedures as all the candidates on the other routes.

Motivation

It is essential that all TAs who approach the route towards gaining HLTA status consider those factors which motivate them. There are many reasons why you may wish to undertake this pathway.

Most experienced TAs like Susan and Angela would identify that their jobs have changed compared with when they started. Susan is completing a Foundation Degree in Teaching and Learning and is using the HLTA status as a stepping stone to her ultimate professional goal of becoming a teacher. She has already identified an ambitious pathway which will ultimately lead her to further qualifications in order to join the teaching profession. Angela and John have not, at present, identified the HLTA as leading to a career move. Indeed, they both see the enhanced status of HLTA as their ultimate work related goal. This, for many professional colleagues, will be sufficient in itself as a motivating factor in undertaking the HLTA pathway. The HLTA is not intended as a stepping stone towards gaining a teaching qualification, though some colleagues may find that it is a useful starting point which can be used towards attaining a place on further training courses which may lead to this goal. Whatever your motivation for embarking on the HLTA, you are beginning a process which will lead to a recognition of your professionalism and will be recognised across educational institutions as an acknowledgement of your skills, knowledge and understanding.

Understanding the HLTA Standards

The HLTA Standards have been designed as a means of assessing your skills, knowledge and understanding as a professional and are divided into 3 sections, these being:

1. Professional Values and Practice 1.1 to 1.6
2. Knowledge and Understanding 2.1 to 2.9
3. Teaching and Learning Activities; these are further subdivided into:
   a) Planning and Expectations 3.1.1 to 3.1.4
   b) Monitoring and Assessment 3.2.1 to 3.2.4
   c) Teaching and Learning Activities 3.3.1 to 3.3.8

You will be aware of these standards if you have begun the application process. It is likely that on viewing these you may feel that some are fairly straightforward while others are more complex. It is probable that some standards will require some clarification. For example, Standard 2.7 is: *They are aware of the statutory frameworks relevant to their role.* With this standard there is a need to specify the extent of the knowledge and understanding expected of TAs working at HLTA level. It is important to specify what is expected of their role and how this expectation will change from, for example, a TA working in a Year 6 class to one working in a nursery school. It is quite probable that you may be more familiar with some of the statutory requirements which relate directly to your current role. For example, if you are working as a TA supporting pupils with special educational needs, you may well feel quite conversant with the Special Educational Needs Code of Practice (DfES 2002b). However, you may be less familiar with other statutory requirements. The important expression in standard 2.7 relates to *frameworks relevant to their role.* There will not be an expectation that you know every piece of educational legislation, but assessors will expect that you can demonstrate an understanding of those which have a direct bearing upon your professional performance.

In the publication *Guidance to the Standards* (TTA 2004) it was noted that:

> Support staff meeting this standard will be able to demonstrate they are aware of the legal framework that underpins teaching and learning, and broader support and protection for both pupils and adults. While it is not necessary to for them to have a detailed knowledge of the whole legal framework they will be aware of their statutory responsibilities and where to gain information, support and assistance when they need it.
>
> (p. 17)

There are, of course, policies and statutes, which relate to critical elements such as child protection, of which all professionals working in schools need to have a good working knowledge. Some standards contain a number of composite statements; for example, Standard 1.1:

> They have high expectations of all pupils; respect their social, cultural, linguistic, religious and ethnic backgrounds; and are committed to raising their educational achievement.

It may be that you work in a situation where there are few, or indeed no children for whom English is an additional language, and that there is little cultural diversity within your school. This cannot to be taken as a reason for not being aware of your responsibilities or for demonstrating your ability to meet this particular standard. It is quite possible that in the future the nature of your school population may change or that having gained your HLTA status you move to a different school with a more diverse population. It is therefore important that you demonstrate that you can meet this standard in full.

Other standards may be specific to your working situation in other ways. For example, Standard 2,2 states that:

> They are familiar with the school curriculum, the age-related expectations of pupils, the main teaching methods and the testing/examination frameworks in the subjects and age ranges in which they are involved.

If you are working in a junior school it is to be expected that you are familiar with the requirements of the National Curriculum for pupils working in Key Stage 2. However, it would be reasonable to expect you to have some understanding of the requirements and content from the National Curriculum at both Key Stages 1 and 3 as there may be pupils in your school who as a result of special educational needs or being gifted or talented may be working outside of the programmes of study for their chronological age. In some instances, in your role as a TA you may be supporting pupils in a specific area of the curriculum such as literacy or numeracy and have little input into other subject-based lessons. You will, however, be expected to demonstrate an understanding of broader curriculum requirements in respect of the age range with which you are working.

Familiarity with the standards is essential if you are to succeed in providing sufficient evidence to go through the assessment process. You should make full use of the *Guidance to the Standards* document, which will clarify interpretation of these and provides some useful exemplars. It is equally important that you seek the advice of experienced colleagues in your school who may be able to provide clarification with regards to school policies and point you in the direction of useful information.

The HLTA Standards are demanding and it would therefore be surprising if you did not find that you needed to improve your work in relation to some of these. This book is intended to provide a broad overview which will assist you in attaining the standards, but cannot act as a substitute for your own efforts in gaining information through your school and by engaging in professional conversation with your colleagues. Clearly, if you are undertaking training related to the HLTA you should receive guidance and support from your tutors. However, as stated in the assessment principles, it is anticipated that you will keep your own detailed records in support of the assessment process.

Summary

- There are three main routes into HLTA and you need to consider carefully which is most appropriate for you.
- The support of your school and colleagues is essential in enabling you to make a smooth progress through this process.
- In order to achieve HLTA status you will need to complete a series of assessments which indicate that you have achieved the standards.

References

Department for Education and Skills (2002) *Time for Standards*. London: DfES

Department for Education and Skills (2002) *Special Educational Needs Code of Practice*. London: DfES

Teacher Training Agency (2004) *Professional Standards for Higher Level Teaching Assistants*. London: TTA

Teacher Training Agency (2004) *Meeting the Professional Standards for the Award of the Higher Level Teaching Assistant Status: Guidance to the Standards*. London TTA

2. Planning, documentation and resources

Introduction

There is a range of documentation that underpins the teaching and learning of English in the primary school. This includes national documents, your school's own policies and schemes of work and published schemes and resources bought in to support teachers and TAs. It is important for you to be able to find and consult the documents that underpin the planning, teaching and learning of English and literacy both nationally and in your school. As a professional TA you will be developing an understanding of the curriculum as a whole and how learning experiences fit together day after day, week after week and term by term to support pupils' progress. Understanding the curriculum as whole will help you develop an awareness of continuity and progression. Your knowledge and understanding of statutory and non-statutory documents and guidance can contribute to your understanding of teachers' planning and teaching. Developing an overview of the English curriculum for your key stage will provide you with an understanding of the bigger picture, allowing you to set individual lessons and sequences of lessons in the context of the learning experience as a whole.

It is probable that some of the documents will be used most directly at specific stages of the planning process rather than be in use on a day-to-day basis in your classroom. We will explore how the available documentation fits together and is used to support effective teaching and learning by teachers and TAs. We will also investigate how your own school uses and interprets this documentation through its own policies, schemes of work and plans. It is likely that you will have encountered other TAs whose schools interpret and apply the same national documents and expectations in a different way to what you experience at your own school. It is important that you begin to understand how your school uses and adapts national documents and guidance to meet the needs of the pupils and families at your school within the school philosophy and ethos.

You will be familiar with working from teachers' planning. Perhaps you are making contributions to this planning and adapting to meet the needs of the individuals and groups you support. You may also be devising your own plans. It is important that you base these on your school's planning approach to ensure consistency for both pupils and staff. Close liaison with the teachers you work with will help you in this. In this chapter we will consider some of effective features of planning in English and literacy.

This chapter will also encourage you to consider the range of support materials and resources used at your school and available through the internet. As a professional TA your contribution of ideas and suggestions from your experience and research can support teaching and learning for the pupils with whom you work. It is likely that you will also have individual knowledge about pupils you work with that will enable you to make a significant contribution to choices about effective learning activities and resources.

In particular, this chapter will focus on the standards in the box below.

HLTA STANDARDS

1.1   They have high expectations of all pupils; respect their social, cultural, linguistic, religious and ethnic backgrounds; and are committed to raising their educational achievement.

1.4   They work collaboratively with colleagues, and carry out their roles effectively, knowing when to seek help and advice.

2.1   They have sufficient understanding of their specialist area to support pupils' learning, and are able to acquire further knowledge to contribute effectively and with confidence to the classes in which they are involved.

2.2   They are familiar with the school curriculum, the age-related expectations of pupils, the main teaching methods and the testing/examination frameworks in the subjects and age ranges in which they are involved.

2.3   They understand the aims, content, teaching strategies and intended outcomes for the lesson in which they are involved, and understand the place of these in the related teaching programme.

2.4   They know how to use ICT to advance pupils' learning, and can use common ICT tools for their own and pupils' benefits.

2.7   They are aware of the statutory frameworks relevant to their role.

3.1.1   They contribute effectively to teachers' planning and preparation of lessons.

3.1.2   Working within a framework set by the teacher, they plan their role in lessons including how they will provide feedback to pupils and colleagues on pupils' learning and behaviour.

3.1.3   They contribute effectively to the selection and preparation of teaching resources that meet the diversity of pupils' needs and interests.

3.3.3   They promote and support the inclusion of all pupils in the learning activities in which they are involved.

3.3.7   They recognise and respond effectively to equal opportunities issues as they arise, including by challenging stereotyped views, and by challenging bullying or harassment, following relevant policies and procedures.

CHAPTER OBJECTIVES

By the end of this chapter you should:

- know more about the official documentation which underpins the teaching and learning of literacy and English in the primary school curriculum

- know more about the school policies and documentation which guide the teaching and learning of literacy at your school

- be aware of the resources that support the teaching and learning of literacy and English at your school

- be able to access and evaluate the range of literacy support materials available to teachers and TAs through the Department for Education and Skills (DfES) and other websites

- understand how the range of documentation and resources fit together to support teaching and learning in your school at the long-, medium- and short-term levels of planning

- be able to contribute to and plan your own role in English and literacy teaching.

Documentation and the stages of planning

The table below outlines each stage of planning, the elements that may be included at each stage and the documents that support the planning of English and literacy at each stage. Schools structure their planning in different ways, with a common difference being the level of detail at the short- and medium-term stages. As a professional TA you should make yourself familiar with how your school organises the planning at each stage. As you do this it is crucial to bear in mind the reason for our planning. As Clarke (1998) states, 'effective planning provides the framework within which we facilitate children's learning'. As you use, adapt and write your own plans you should remember that ensuring children learn is the purpose for your work.

STAGE	MAY INCLUDE	ENGLISH AND LITERACY DOCUMENTATION
Long-term planning / curriculum map	Coverage of a year or key stage Indication of breadth and balance of subjects, the content, continuity and progression in each subject, and links between subjects Allocation of time for teaching and assessment	*The National Curriculum Handbook for Primary Teachers*

▶

Medium-term planning, unit plans, schemes of work	Learning objectives Content organised into coherent units Learning outcomes Opportunities to develop key aspects of learning Links and references to other subjects/units of work	*The National Literacy Strategy. Framework for Teaching.* *Speaking, Listening and Learning.* *The Literacy Planning CD-ROM.*
Short-term planning, weekly, daily or lesson plans	Learning objectives and success criteria for the lesson Key vocabulary Strategies for differentiation Organisational details such as resources, timings, use of adults, range of teaching strategies Class and group targets Assessment notes made during and after teaching	Published and school resources.

You may wish to annotate this table according to your own school's policy. A more detailed coverage of the key elements of planning and the planning processes can be found in 'Planning and assessment for learning. Designing opportunities for learning' part of the *Excellence and Enjoyment* materials (DfES 2004b).

National documentation (statutory)

The National Curriculum Handbook for Primary Teachers in England (1999) sets out the legal requirements of the National Curriculum (NC) in England for pupils aged 5 to 11 years old. This document establishes entitlement and standards, and promotes continuity, coherence and public understanding. It outlines values, aims and purposes for the whole school curriculum.

PRACTICAL TASK

Track down a copy of *The National Curriculum Handbook* in your school. Alternatively you can find it online at **www.nc.uk.net**.

Identify and read the following:

- values, aims and purposes (pp. 10–13)

- the school curriculum and the National Curriculum (pp. 16–23)

- structure (pp. 26–27)

- general teaching requirements (pp. 26–40).

Consider these sections in relation to the teaching and learning of English at your school.

In addition to general information, *The National Curriculum Handbook* outlines the programmes of study for each subject at Key Stages 1 and 2. The programme of study for English is divided into three attainment targets:

En1 Speaking and listening
En2 Reading
En3 Writing.

Within each attainment target there are two sections:

knowledge, skills and understanding
breadth of study.

This programme of study forms the basis for teachers' planning across the year and key stage. If you have the opportunity to talk with the teachers you work with, you could discuss when they use this information in the planning process. It is likely that they use it as part of long-term planning.

At the back of the handbook is a booklet which sets out of level descriptions within each attainment target. These describe the type and range of performance that pupils working at each level would typically demonstrate. These, along with other support and guidance materials, provide the basis for assessments. This will be considered further in subsequent chapters.

PRACTICAL TASK

Read the programme of study for English for the key stage in which you work:

- teaching requirements for English (pp. 42–58)
- the NC attainment targets for English (pp. 3–7 in the back).

Identify the following parts:

- attainment targets
- knowledge, skills and understanding
- breadth of study
- level descriptions.

Consider how this information relates to the planning you work with.

Look at En3 Writing breadth of study (11) for either Key Stage 1 or Key Stage 2.

This statement outlines the audiences for writing that pupils should encounter throughout the key stage.

Which have you encountered with the pupils you work with this year?

Some opportunities or audiences might occur outside English lessons in cross-curricular contexts.

Consult your school's long-term plan or curriculum map for the year or key stage to identify how and when the pupils will experience them in the future.

Are there any notable gaps?

KEY STAGE 1 – En3 11. RANGE OF READERS FOR WRITING	SO FAR THIS YEAR / KEY STAGE		DURING THE REST OF THIS YEAR/KEY STAGE
	IN ENGLISH OR LITERACY LESSON	IN THE REST OF THE CURRICULUM	
Teachers			
Pupils			
Other adults			
The writers themselves			
KEY STAGE 2 – En3 11. RANGE OF READERS FOR WRITING			
Teachers			
The class			
Other pupils			
Adults			
The wider community			
Imagined readers			

National documentation (non-statutory)

In 1998 the National Literacy Strategy (NLS) Framework for teaching was introduced to primary schools. This document sets out teaching objectives for reading and writing in Years Reception to 6. In Years 1 to 6 the teaching objectives are set out for each term. Teaching objectives are organised as strands:

- Word level – phonics, spelling, vocabulary and handwriting
- Sentence level – grammar and punctuation
- Text level – comprehension and composition.

In addition, the range of fiction, poetry and non-fiction is outlined for each term. It is recommended that a minimum of 75 per cent of the term's reading and writing should be from within this range. There is potential for making strong cross-curricular links with the non-fiction part of the range. The range links back to the forms of writing specified in the breadth-of-study section in each attainment target in the NC document.

In 2003 *Speaking, Listening and Learning* provided termly objectives for speaking and listening. These are organised in four strands:

- Speaking
- Listening
- Group discussion and interaction
- Drama.

These should be used in conjunction with the NLS objectives for reading and writing. You may find it useful to copy the speaking and listening termly objectives, cut them up and clip or stick them to the appropriate NLS pages for ease of reference.

In addition, to this, recent DfES guidance through *The Literacy Planning CD-ROM*, distributed to schools in 2004, introduced the unit plan. The unit plan format helps teachers to do the following:

- Assemble text, sentence and word objectives in coherent units.
- Identify which objectives will be taught discretely, which integrated.
- Identify which objectives will recur and be built upon.
- Indicate texts used.
- Indicate pupil outcomes.
- Indicate speaking and listening objectives.
- Make explicit and meaningful links to other areas of the curriculum/ events, etc.

It is assumed that the teacher will be reading other texts to the class on a regular basis outside the literacy hour.

(DfES 2004a)

PRACTICAL TASK

- Use a copy of The NLS Framework for teaching. There are copies in every school. It can also be accessed online at **www.standards.dfes.gov.uk/primary/literacy.**

- Read the objectives for the current term.

- Get a copy of your year group's current medium-term plan or unit plans for English or literacy.

- Consider how the NLS objectives are organised in the planning you work with. This may a set of unit plans or one medium-term plan.

- Notice where some recur each week (continuous) and some appear once for a concentrated period of time (blocked).

- Notice the links between literacy objectives and learning in other areas of the curriculum.

- Talk with a teacher about the rationale behind how the NLS objectives are organised into a teaching programme for the half term for the year group or class you work with.

You may find that the objectives are organised in relation to cross-curricular opportunities, school events, available resources, other or a combination of these factors.

School documentation

In addition to national statutory information and non-statutory guidance your own school will have documents which set out its individual philosophy and practices in relation to teaching and learning in English. There may be a specific policy for the teaching of English, or a teaching and learning policy with references to general issues and specific curriculum areas. As a professional TA supporting the teaching and learning of English you should read this school-specific guidance to ensure that you understand the underlying philosophy that your school has agreed upon. When you read this it is likely that you will be able to make connections between the practice you see in the classroom and the policy statements. Given the amount of documentation and guidance schools receive, you may also notice differences between the school policies and guidance and the practice you are experiencing. Schools tend to address this gap through regular review of policies as their practice evolves in response to the drive to improve.

There other sources of information which may also be relevant to the planning, teaching and learning of English in your school. These may include:

- Immediate priorities for staff professional development linked to recent inspection findings, school improvement plan priorities or local and national initiatives.
- The need or desire to use new resources from national agencies or publishers, or schemes to support teaching and learning in specific areas of English (for example, spelling) or for specific groups of pupils (for example, pupils who need additional support with reading).
- Ongoing changes in schools. You will need to be alert to these, as changes have an impact on school priorities and classroom practice. If you are able to attend school training sessions, staff meetings or read minutes or outcomes from these sessions, this will help you keep up to date with your school's situation.

PRACTICAL TASK

Use a copy of the school's English policy and other school-specific documentation.

- Make a note of five of the aims or priorities for the teaching and learning of English at your school.
- Consider how you have seen these put into action in the classrooms where you work.
- Consider how you contribute to putting these into action in your work with teachers and pupils.
- Talk with a teacher about your findings.

An example is included to get you started:

AIMS	EXAMPLES IN CLASSROOM PRACTICE	IN MY ROLE...
To ensure pupils have opportunities to develop confidence in using their speaking skills	Regular opportunities for pupils as individuals, in small groups and with whole class to speak in front of audiences such as their own class, several classes, the whole school, parents and visitors.	I praise pupils who speak up confidently in groups, the class or in assembly. I support pupils by giving them the chance to practise what they are going to say and giving them positive and formative feedback.

Planning

Planning at the short-term stage, the plans we work from during the lesson, are the key documents that support your role as a professional TA in the classroom. Your experience of planning will range from working with plans supplied to you by teachers, adapting these plans, making contributions to planning and planning your own lessons and sequences of lessons working within the framework set by the teacher you work with. Your role in planning may depend on the approach your school takes. The way schools design their planning formats varies enormously. It is important that you can identify and understand the key features of planning that support effective teaching and learning.

Common sense and good practice would suggest that you, and all the adult working in the classroom in a lesson, should have a copy of the planning in advance of the lesson. This will give you the opportunity to become familiar with the lesson, reflect on your role within it and make appropriate preparation. In real life sometimes systems set up to share planning can be overtaken by workload and circumstances. As part of your role as a professional TA you must be prepared to take an active role in collecting and copying plans rather than waiting for a teacher to issue them to you. You should also be aware that plans should and do change in response to the pupils' learning and progress, so as the week goes on you may need to check for changes with the teacher or suggest changes you feel would be appropriate from your work with the pupils.

Some important general features relation to planning for teaching and learning have been discussed in chapter 3 of *Becoming a Primary Higher Level Teaching Assistant* (Rose 2005). When planning for the teaching and learning of English or literacy there are some specific factors to consider. We have considered long- and medium-term planning in relation to the documents teachers use to support this. Many schools use the NLS Framework and unit plans as the basis for the planning and teaching of literacy and English. Some schools have adapted them to fit their own needs and priorities but it is likely that you will see objectives and organisational features from the NLS occurring on the short-term plans that you work with and from. These may include a clear identification of text, sentence and word level work and a lesson structured around main teaching, guided group and independent work and concluding with a plenary session. Short-term planning may be presented as a weekly, daily or lesson plan. Again this will vary from school to school or in relation to the needs of teachers, TAs and the pupils.

Case study

Sharmila is a TA supporting pupils in literacy lessons in a Year 2 class. She receives the teacher's planning a week in advance although she knows the general outline from the medium-term plan. In order to clarify her role in the lesson Sharmila annotates the planning with questions and points to follow up herself or with the teacher before the lesson.

	Monday 22 Sept (T and TA)
9.05 Word level Intro	**LI – To discriminate the long i sound in words. i-e igh y** Give chn yes/no cards. Read a list of mixed words. Chn hold up 'yes' if they can hear the phoneme in the word. Ext – where in the word is the phoneme? start/middle/end – say some words segment and synthesise.

Which children should I sit with to support?
Could I see the list of words?
Are there any children who need to practise this first?

9.20 Sentence/ text level Main teaching	Look at the cover – author/title/ illustrator Ask chn to predict what the story might be about from the cover – support chn to say ideas in sentences – practise to friend first. **RC4 – To understand time and sequential relationships in stories** Read the story *Cleversticks* Bernard Ashley. Chn should listen and try to recall events which we will recount after. Talk through main events – use picturess to support ordering. Key questions – What happened next/before/after? Model developing sentences and write one together to start.	Read the story and note main events. Which children should I sit with to support?
WAL WWNT	**We are learning to** To put events from a story in order **We will need to** Order 3, 4 or 6 pictures from the story. Write a sentence about each one. Check from what we know about the story that the order is right.	Check that the children I support understand the word 'events'

Groups	Red Working at level 1A and 2C TA	Blue Working at level 1C and 1B T	Yellow Working at Level 1C T

Notes for teacher, TA	Sequence 6 pics Write just the sentences. Remind the children to use full stops and capital letters.	Sequence 3 or 4 pics. Stick them down. Construct and write a sentence for each one with help – say the sentence to an adult or friend to check it makes sense.	Recap on LI and success criteria before the activity. Use the time words throughout, prompt children to use them, note who uses them spontaneously. Ask children to explain how they know the placing of events is correct.

10.10 Plenary	Review WWNT... hands up/examples from groups. Children to articulate *how* they sequenced – with reference to the story, makes sense. Mix up the pictures and ask children to identify the errors with reference to the story. Encourage use of words – before, next, after, the next day, suddenly, then etc.	Which children should I support?

In the case study above the TA has had time to reflect upon her role in the lesson. She has identified parts of the lesson where her role is not clear and will be able to follow these up with the teacher. One way of addressing this is for the TA and teacher to agree upon her role in parts of the lesson such as the main teaching or plenary and then agree that she will perform this role unless the plan specifies something different. We can also see that Sharmila is alert to the teacher's clear, shared learning intentions and success criteria and is prepared to use these with her group. She has also anticipated some points of learning where she might take notes and report back to the teacher. Sharmila might also annotate the plan as the teacher is teaching in response to any on-the-spot changes the teacher makes in relation to the pupils' responses.

There are parts of the lesson where attention tends to be focused on the teacher at the front of the class. Professional TAs can sometimes feel that they are in a somewhat passive or at best reactive role during this time. It is important to work with the class teacher to clarify your role during these parts of the lesson, usually the main teaching and plenary sections. It may be that your role has a particular dimension that will focus your support on pupils with special educational needs or pupils who are learning English as additional language. In these cases it is likely your focus will be related to the individual education plans or support programmes for these pupils.

At a more general level, developing an agreed and specific role with the teacher for you will result in using your professional skills fully to support pupils' learning. This might be indicated to you on the lesson planning, in planning meetings or through ongoing professional conversations. You might consider trying some of the following:

- Observing, assessing or noting the participation of an identified pupil or pupils in turn over the weeks or half-terms.
- Providing and using matching resources for pupils who find it hard to focus on a large text/activities at the front.
- Reiterating and confirming learning objectives and teaching points.
- Encouraging pupils' participation through confirming answers before they volunteer them or rehearsing contributions to the plenary within the group teaching part of the lesson.
- Picking up on inattentiveness and refocusing pupils' attention in a quiet and subtle manner.
- Modelling teacher expectations, for example, in active listening, reading with expression or explicitly following the text.
- Planned 'joining in' – where you model responses or questions that you have agreed with the teacher before the lesson.
- Planned 'doing it wrongly' – where you and the teacher have agreed that one of you will demonstrate a mistake or misconception that needs to be addressed with the pupils.
- Supporting the teacher in evaluating the impact and success of the teaching by giving feedback on pupils' responses.

As you move towards planning your own lessons, or activities within lessons, the teachers' plans and the school approach to planning are the model you should follow. As a professional TA you will use your experience and professional judgement as to how much detail you need to ensure the pupils you teach learn and make progress in your lessons. Working closely with the class teacher, being involved in the planning sessions and asking for feedback on your planning will also help you develop your expertise in this area.

Resources for teaching

Resources to support you in planning

Since the publication of the NLS, additional guidance materials have been provided to schools relating to specific aspects of the curriculum include 'Grammar for writing' and 'Playing with sounds'. Other materials support the teaching and learning of identified groups of pupils include 'Additional literacy support' and 'Early literacy support'. We will look more closely at these in subsequent chapters.

In addition to the resources that you have in your school there are many resources and support materials available online. As part of your role as professional TA you are undoubtedly developing your own ICT skills. Effective use of internet sources can support you in your role and allow you to draw upon a wider range of resources than immediately available to you in your school.

Some of the major sources of support materials are:

- **www.standards.dfes.gov.uk/primary/literacy**
  From this web page you can access the NLS Framework for teaching, latest teaching resources and plans, case studies and publications.
- **www.qca.org.uk**
- **www.nc.uk.net**
- **www.bbc.co.uk/schools/**
  From this web page you can access support materials for a range of television and radio programmes.

Resources to help you in teaching

Each school has a wide variety of resources used to support teaching and learning in English. As a professional TA you may be familiar with the resources used regularly in your classroom or in relation to the needs of the children that you support. It may be that maintaining resources is an aspect of your role as a TA. It is useful for you to develop an overall awareness of all the resources available in your school. This will allow you to support teachers effectively and make appropriate suggestions and decisions about choice of resources for the class and for pupils you are working with.

PRACTICAL TASK

- Choose one area of English (such as speaking and listening, spelling, handwriting).

- Investigate the resources available in school that are used to support teaching and learning in this area.

- Use the chart to make notes:

ASPECT OF ENGLISH	RESOURCES (name, brief description)	LOCATION (in your classroom, in other classrooms, held centrally, etc.)
NLS support materials		
Published support materials		
ICT resources – software, videos and DVDs, tapes etc.		
Concrete resources for use with pupils		
Games		
'made' and 'found' resources		

- Consider which resources you use regularly and which you might consider using in the future.

Evaluating resources

While it is important to be aware of the range of resources available in schools for the teaching and learning of English, it is also important to evaluate them before use. There are occasions when resources are distracting and take pupils' concentration away from the learning objective. There are a number of factors we must take into consideration when we choose the resources that support out teaching. These include the following.

Fitness for purpose

Does the resource support pupils in meeting the learning objective? Are there enough for pupils to share realistically and prevent squabbling?

How much time will be spent giving out and collecting the resource?

Will this have a negative impact on the learning?

Quality

Is the resource attractive and motivating?

Is it complete and robust enough to survive use by a class or group of pupils?

Is the resource appropriate to the social, cultural, linguistic, religious and ethnic background of the pupils?

Finally, you may find it useful to have your own copies of some of these documents and resources. Many publications are available to download. Some can be requested through your school.

DOCUMENTS	DO YOU HAVE ACCESS TO IT?	DO YOU HAVE YOUR OWN COPY OF IT?
The National Curriculum Handbook for Primary Teachers in England		
The National Literacy Strategy Framework for Teaching		
The Literacy Planning CD-ROM		
Speaking, Listening and Learning		
School English policy		
Other relevant school policies		
School long-term plan or curriculum map		
School medium-term planning		
School short-term planning		
Any published resource materials		
Other useful resources available in your school		

Summary

Understanding and using planning effectively is supported by:

- Awareness of and reference to the English and literacy documentation at national, local and school level.
- Awareness of changes and updates to national documentation and research. Using the internet can help you to access resources and guidance.
- Obtaining planning before the lesson and reflecting upon and clarifying your role within it. Close liaison with the teacher will help with this.
- Knowledge of and critical evaluation of resources to support the learning of the individuals, groups and classes you work with.

References

Clarke, S. (1998) *Targeting Assessment in the Primary School*. London: Hodder and Stoughton

Department for Education and Employment (1998) *The National Literacy Strategy Framework for Teaching*. London: DfEE

Department for Education and Employment (1999) *The National Curriculum Handbook for Primary Teachers in England*. London: DfEE

Department for Education and Skills (2003) *Speaking, Listening and Learning*. London: DfES

Department for Education and Skills (2004a) *The Literacy Planning CD-ROM*. London: DfES

Department for Education and Skills (2004b) *Excellence and Enjoyment: Learning and Teaching in the Primary Years*. London: DfES

Rose, R. (2005) *Becoming a Primary Higher Level Teaching Assistant*. Exeter: Learning Matters

Watkinson, A. (2002) *Assisting Learning and Supporting Teaching*. London: David Fulton Publishers

3. Speaking and listening

Introduction

Becoming a confident and articulate speaker and an active and purposeful listener are essential skills for children in both learning and social situations. From your own experience of working in primary classrooms, you will be aware of how of how often pupils are asked to make oral contributions in group and whole-class situations and listen to each other and to adults in order to learn and participate in classroom life. Perhaps a part of your role involves you in supporting pupils who find aspects of speaking and listening, socially and/or academically challenging.

In the National Curriculum all three attainment targets in English have equal status and importance. It is clearly stated that planned learning experiences should integrate speaking and listening, reading and writing. The absence of termly learning objectives in the NLS Framework may have led to a focus on reading and writing in recent years. The QCA guidance *Speaking, Listening and Learning*, issued in 2003, addressed this imbalance by providing termly objectives in each of the four strands of speaking and listening. It is likely that in the future as the current NLS is revised, the speaking and listening objectives will be incorporated directly into the Framework.

In this chapter we will consider how teachers organise their classrooms to provide a supportive environment for the development of speaking and listening skills. As a professional TA your role in maintaining and contributing to this is significant. We will also consider performance from Year 1 to Year 6 in order to develop an understanding of progression. This will engage you investigating planning and differentiation. We will explore the planning of learning experiences to teach specific skills. We will investigate the opportunities for using speaking and listening skills purposefully in English, in other subject areas and in 'real-life' contexts including out-of-school contexts. Assessing speaking and listening can be challenging. This chapter will examine your role in the assessment of pupils' speaking and listening skills.

In particular, this chapter will focus on the standards in the box overleaf.

A supportive classroom for speaking and listening

As an adult you will probably have been in situations where you felt able to join in conversation or discussion confidently and other situations where you felt less confident and therefore less likely to join in. Goodwin (2001) has emphasised the need for us to value all children's contributions and ensure that we include all children. Given the importance of speaking and listening for learning, it is vital that we provide children with the most supportive environment for speaking and listening that we can. In classrooms where pupils are speaking confidently and listening purposely in a range of contexts, it is likely that there is an underlying philosophy and a shared set of conventions.

HLTA STANDARDS

1.1 They have high expectations of all pupils; respect their social, cultural, linguistic, religious and ethnic backgrounds; and are committed to raising their educational achievement.

2.5 They know the key factors that can affect the way pupils learn.

2.9 They know a range of strategies to establish a purposeful learning environment and to promote good behaviour.

3.1.1 They contribute effectively to teachers' planning and preparation of lessons.

3.1.2 Working within a framework set by the teacher, they plan their role in lessons including how they will provide feedback to pupils and colleagues on pupils' learning and behaviour.

3.1.3 They contribute effectively to the selection and preparation of teaching resources that meet the diversity of pupils' needs and interests.

3.1.4 They are able to contribute to the planning of opportunities for pupils to learn in out-of-school contexts, in accordance with school policies and procedures.

3.3.1 Using clearly structured teaching and learning activities, they interest and motivate pupils, and advance their learning.

3.3.2 They communicate effectively and sensitively with pupils to support their learning.

3.3.3 They promote and support the inclusion of all pupils in the learning activities in which they are involved.

3.3.5 They advance pupils' learning in a range of classroom settings, including working with individuals, small groups and whole classes where the assigned teacher is not present.

3.3.7 They recognise and respond effectively to equal opportunities issues as they arise, including by challenging stereotyped views, and by challenging bullying or harassment, following relevant policies and procedures.

CHAPTER OBJECTIVES

By the end of this chapter you should:

● have considered the factors that support pupils in developing their speaking and listening skills

● investigated the planning of speaking and listening skills in the lessons which you work

● have considered the range of teaching strategies you can use for developing pupils' speaking and listening skills in English lessons, across the curriculum, in out-of-school contexts and in day-to-day school life.

In many classrooms, at the start of the year, the teacher and pupils will talk through and agree the classroom rules and conventions that will ensure that the classroom is a purposeful, secure and happy learning environment. Speaking and listening will be an aspect of this. Decisions may be made about how pupils take turns, indicate they want to answer questions, the volume of their voice, how they show they are listening and more. It is important that any conventions devised are agreed by all the pupils and adults working in the pupils and put into practice consistently, referred to, revised where appropriate and used as a basis for praise. They can be especially useful in classrooms where several teachers and TAs teach the same pupils at different times. As a professional TA you might be involved in helping pupils formulate and express their ideas in a positive form. For example, 'Don't interrupt' can be remodelled as 'Remember to listen to the person who is talking'. You can use the agreed conventions as a basis for expectations when working with a group by reminding before you start. They can also form the basis of giving specific praise. For example, 'I liked the way you listened until Jenny has finished talking' or 'the questions you asked Iqbal showed me that you listened carefully to what he said'.

If you were not able to be involved in developing conventions it is important that you make yourself aware of them so that you can be consistent with the pupils. Many classrooms have their rules or conventions pinned up around the classroom. If they are not apparent you should ask the class teacher to ensure that you can support the teacher and pupils in a manner consistent with the usual expectations. If you are able to use consistent rules and conventions that the pupils are used to, this can support positive behaviour.

You might find it useful to watch the Year 4 term 1 extract 'Celts and Romans' on the *Speaking, Listening and Learning* video. This shows a pupils reviewing their ground rules for effective dialogue to ensure that they have a shared understanding, for use later in a history context. Poster 4 from *Speaking, Listening, Learning: Working with Children who have SEN* outlines in detail factors related to acoustics, space, lighting, feelings and visual prompts in the classroom environment. Although some of these factors may be beyond your control, an understanding of those that you can modify in order to support pupils' learning is part of your role as a professional TA.

PRACTICAL TASK

Investigate the rules or conventions for speaking and listening in one of the classrooms where you work.

Make a copy of the existing rules or make notes of what you think they are from your experience in the classroom.

Ask the pupils to tell you about the rules relating to speaking and listening as they understand them.

Do their ideas and understanding match what you found out?

Notice how the rules or conventions are used in practice:

- Are the pupils praised in relation to them?
- Are the rules revisited and revised when appropriate?
- Are they used consistently by everyone in the classroom?
- Do the rules take account of the individual needs in the class?

How do you use them to guide your work with individuals, groups and the class?

You should also consider your role as a model for pupils. You might consider how you use your own speaking and listening skills. For example, how do you show the pupils that you are listening to them? You probably look at the child who is talking, nod and encourage them to continue and make your reply relevant to what they said. When you are chatting to the pupils about school life and personal topics, perhaps your language and tone are more informal than if you are leading an activity in a science lesson. Being a appropriate model of the speaking and listening skills we are teaching on a day-to-day basis is important, especially when you are called upon to be more explicit about these skills or break them down into smaller steps to support pupils. Consideration of this aspect of your role might lead you to think about your own use of vocabulary, sentence construction and expression.

Planning for speaking and listening

Speaking, Listening and Learning (2003) summarises the four strands of speaking and listening as:

- *Speaking*: being able to speak clearly and to develop and sustain ideas in talk.
- *Listening*: developing active listening strategies and critical skills of analysis.
- *Group discussion and interaction*: taking different roles in groups, making a range of contributions and working collaboratively.
- *Drama*: improvising and working in role, scripting and performing, and responding to performances.

Learning objectives for each term in each of the four strands are outlined in detail within the QCA materials. You may find it useful to copy them and attach them to the relevant pages in the NLS Framework so that you can make clear and relevant links between speaking and listening, reading and writing for the term. Links should also be made to other areas of the curriculum and school activities where pupils can have the opportunity to use their speaking and listening skills in purposeful contexts. This is likely to happen at the medium-term planning stage. Opportunities to use skills in a variety of contexts in school life or out-of-school contexts should also be integrated.

As well as your immediate objectives for the week and half term it is useful to be familiar with the speaking and listening attainment target En1 for your key stage and the termly objectives for the year in which you work. This will give you a useful overview to help you to support or extend pupils. As a professional TA you will be aware of the importance of clear and thorough planning in order to support effective learning. You may regularly use and contribute to teachers' planning. It can be very useful for you to look at the general class planning and consider it in relation to your role in the lesson. This will allow you think through and anticipate any aspects of the lesson where you may need to supply specific support, adapt resources or clarify aspects with the teacher before the lesson.

Case study

Alan is a TA working in a class of Year 2 pupils. In a forthcoming lesson the teacher has asked him to support a group of six higher-ability pupils.

The Year 2 term 2 objective is:

17. To tell real and imagined stories using the conventions of familiar story language.

Looking at the teacher's planning for the literacy session on storytelling and using his experience of the group, Alan anticipates that his group will meet the learning objectives and success criteria with ease. Alan consults the Speaking, Listening and Learning *objectives and identifies the next time the objective occurs. He identifies 'using appropriate expression, tone and volume' as an additional area he can focus on with the group in order to extend their learning. Alan discusses this suggestion with the teacher who agrees that this differentiation will be appropriate to the group.*

Alan plans his approach to ensure that his group meet the whole-class objectives and success criteria before moving on to the extension activity. He adds some notes to his copy of the plan to remind him what to do and ensures that he follows the teacher's method of sharing learning objectives and discussing success criteria, an approach that the pupils are familiar with. As the lesson progresses Alan is able to challenge the group to use their voices expressively, making connections with their reading aloud. This ensures that the group remain purposefully on task throughout this part of the lesson.

In this case study we can see that Alan has used his knowledge of the pupils and the existing planning to make a professional judgement about the pupils' learning. He uses the available documentation to make suggestions about how to extend the learning experience along the same strand of the speaking objectives. It is significant that he confirms his thinking with the class teacher and frames the extension work in the same terms as the teacher. This is one possibility for differentiating the learning. Alternatively Alan could have considered making a link to other objectives from the same year and term but in a different strand, such as drama or listening. Alan's contribution has ensured that the group work purposefully on task, pre-empting the possibility of the group completing the task quickly and becoming distracted.

Strategies to develop speaking and listening

There are many strategies and activities that can be used to develop speaking and listening. Your school may be using the *Speaking, Listening and Learning* materials that have been in school since 2003. There are other published resources that your school may use. As you work in classrooms you will also get an idea of what works effectively from your observations of teachers and pupils.

In the case study below Karen is given the opportunity to investigate a concern both she and the teacher have. Karen is able to use her presence at the whole-class teaching time to observe Jasmin over a short time as a basis for planning support. The discussion of Karen's findings lead to a planned change in the way the teacher and TA approach the way all the pupils make contributions at whole-class teaching time, incorporating ideas from recent training. Karen is able to develop her role at whole-class time by being a supportive partner to some pupils who find 'think, pair, share' a challenge at first. By working together effectively to meet the needs of one pupil, Karen and the teacher have implemented a strategy that will contribute to a positive environment for speaking and listening for all the pupils. This strategy could be used by a bilingual assistant to support pupils who might benefit from trying out their contribution in their first language before contributing in English.

Case study

Jasmin is a Year 2 pupil who is learning English as an additional language (EAL). Her conversational English is developing well and she participates fully in small-group work. The class teacher and Karen, the TA in the classroom, have begun to feel that Jasmin is reluctant to contribute in whole-class situations. Karen observes Jasmin in the whole-class teaching part of literacy lessons for about a week. She notices that if Jasmin can check out her answer with someone near her (child or adult) she is more likely to take the risk and put her hand up to join in. Karen and the class teacher speculate about whether this is a strategy that could be actively promoted to support several of the pupils. The class teacher has recently encountered 'think, pair, share' suggested in Speaking, Listening and Learning. *At the start of the following week the class are introduced to this idea. Before answering questions or making comments in whole-class teaching time, the pupils are encouraged to think briefly on their own, then turn to the child next to them, pair up and talk quietly about their idea for a short time before the teacher asks for contributions to be shared with the class. Karen is involved in modelling this with some of the pupils at whole-class time. After a few weeks it is apparent that Jasmin is volunteering to make contributions more frequently and with more animation. Some of the other pupils in the class are also making more confident contributions.*

Giving an opportunity to rehearse ideas before they contribute them to the class can support pupils who are hesitant or need longer to organise their thoughts. This can be structured through paired work or by allowing for 'wait time', a longer pause after a question has been asked by the teacher or TA. You will have noticed that where a teacher asks quick-fire questions that require an instant response, not all pupils can supply an answer at such a pace and some pupils do not participate. The type of question that elicits this instant response tends to be that of straightforward recall questions. When a deeper and more considered response is required, increasing the wait time to three or more seconds can allow pupils time to think through their response, resulting in more responses of better quality.

Imaginative play, storytelling and drama also contribute towards a varied and creative speaking and listening curriculum and allow us to make links with reading, writing and other areas of the curriculum. They allow us to create imaginative contexts in which to speak and listen that we could not provide in our day-to-day classrooms, such as the chance to be in role as a story character, doing someone's job, participating in a historic event or as a visitor to a distant place. Imaginative play, storytelling and drama are experiences that should be available for all pupils up to Year 6 (and beyond), though the first two tend to be more apparent at Foundation and Key Stage 1.

There are a number of useful teaching strategies outlined on the poster entitled 'Group discussion and interaction' in *Speaking, Listening and Learning* (2003). You may wish to explore these for use in English lessons and across the curriculum.

Speaking and listening across the curriuclum

There are many opportunities for pupils to use and apply their speaking and listening skills in areas of the curriculum other than English or literacy lessons. It is important for pupils to be able to use their skills purposefully in all their learning. Being clear about the learning objectives in the curriculum area and in speaking and listening will allow you provide effective support for learners. It can be helpful to look at the planning and think through any issues in relation to speaking and listening for the pupils you are supporting. You need to be clear about the subject-specific vocabulary that the pupils need to understand and use in their discussion and writing. You might also consider particular ways of expressing their ideas, specific sentence structures and expressions that they will encounter.

As a professional TA you will be developing a range of strategies to support pupils in this situation. It is likely that some of these strategies will have been built in at the planning stage. Many teachers present key vocabulary on cards or lists so that new words and phrases are clear and available. Depending on the needs of the pupils you support, pictures, real objects or symbols might be added. Part of your role might be to introduce some important vocabulary to some pupils before the lesson to give them a chance to rehearse new words in a secure and supportive setting. You might follow up the lesson with some conversations to clarify whether pupils do understand and are able to use the words and phrases appropriately. This can inform future planning for individuals, groups and the class.

PRACTICAL TASK

Choose a short-term plan for a subject other than English that you are currently working with.

Identify the vocabulary that the pupils will need to be able to understand, respond to and use in order to participate in the lesson.

Identify sentence constructions or expressions that pupils will need to be able to understand, respond to and use.

Consider the strategies you could use to support pupils in learning and using the vocabulary and sentence structures in their work.

Many early years and Key Stage 1 classrooms contain an imaginative play area. This 'pretend' environment, the resources and play encouraged within it can supply some great opportunities for developing the drama strand of speaking and listening. Planning what the play area will be like, the resources available to pupils, what adults will do to develop language in the play and how learning objectives in areas of the curriculum may be met in the play area are crucial.

In the case study presented opposite, we can see how an imaginative play area has strong links to the pupils' learning in the literacy lessons and the role of the professional TA enhances this in a number of ways. Vanessa contributes to the setting up, changing and maintaining of the area. She works with pupils to develop their play and their language. She can, from time to time, observe the pupils and assess and evaluate their play. This experience also has potential to be a meaningful context for writing.

The case study is an example of an imaginary environment. Imaginative play areas also offer scope for pupils to research a more 'real' environment and the people who work there such as a garage, garden centre or café. This can be the basis of some valuable and exciting learning experiences for pupils at Key Stages 1 and 2. Although very few older pupils tend to have the opportunity to learn in this kind of way, creative and careful planning linking speaking and listening, reading and writing and other areas of the curriculum such as history and geography can provide a motivating learning experience.

Speaking and listening in out-of-school contexts

Giving pupils opportunities to use their speaking and listening skills in 'real-life' situations gives them a sense of purpose and an understanding of their learning in a way it is impossible to recreate in a classroom. Visits to

Case study

Vanessa is a TA in a Year 1 classroom. In term 2 the imaginative play corner is a cottage in the middle of a forest. The pupils have been involved in making the environment. They have painted trees, printed the walls of the cottage, and collected items to go in there. In literacy the pupils have been reading and exploring a range of traditional tales such as Little Red Riding Hood, Goldilocks *and* The Little Red Hen. *Each week Vanessa changes the cottage slightly to fit each story. Working with the teacher she plans a drama activity to support the pupils' learning in literacy. The speaking and listening objective is:*

Year 1 term 2
8 To act out well-known stories using different voices for characters.

This links with text objectives 4 and 9 from the NLS. When working with groups Vanessa supports the pupils to role-play episodes from the story, encouraging them to use some of the words the characters use in the story. She joins in to help develop, sustain and extend the pupils' play, sometimes assuming the role of a character from the story. Over time Vanessa also uses the opportunity to observe the pupils' use of language, recall of the stories and social interaction.

places outside school, participating in events and occasions or inviting visitors into school enrich pupils' learning and often provide motivation and inspiration. Given the amount of time and effort that it takes to plan and organise these experiences, it is vital that we are clear about what we plan for pupils to learn and that we prepare them for the learning experience fully.

In the case study overleaf we can see the importance of the TA's research about the visit. By visiting the website she was able to anticipate some of the vocabulary and question types that the pupils would encounter. By working with the teacher at the planning stage they were able to address the subject-specific vocabulary so that the pupils would have some familiarity before their visit. Anna was also able to support some pupils by practising the question types and responses with them to boost their confidence and familiarity. This resulted in their engagement and participation in the gallery session. This type of preparation could also have been conducted through a pre-visit appointment at the art gallery where Anna and the teacher could have discussed the session with the curator or observed a session to help them plan their preparation for the visit. A pre-visit can also give you the opportunity to brief the person leading the session on the specific needs of the pupils. Museum and gallery curators and teachers are usually happy to adapt their sessions to the needs of your pupils.

Case study

Anna is a TA working with a Year 4 class. The teacher is planning a visit to the local art gallery to look at the sculpture collection with a particular focus on sculptures of people. Before the visit Anna looks at the website to look at some of the sculptures and the supporting information presented with them. She identifies a number of words that she feels the pupils will find challenging. Anna talks with the teacher about the objectives for the visit. They consider the vocabulary it is likely that the pupils will need in order to access the gallery session. Anna makes key vocabulary cards for use with the whole-class and a supplementary set with picture, photo and symbol clues. These include words such as 'abstract', 'representational', 'bust', 'figure', etc. She also collects a set of materials that the pupils will encounter such as wood, bronze, stone so that the pupils can touch them to appreciate the tactile qualities of the sculpture materials since it is likely that the pupils will not be allowed to touch the sculptures. Finally Anna and the teacher consider the question types that pupils will be asked to respond to. These include open questions where pupils will be asked to express and justify their opinion or describe their feelings in relation to the art work. Anna is aware that for some of the pupils in the class this will be challenging. She suggests to the teacher that she work with this group to rehearse this type of talk at school before the visit.

The visit goes well, with the pupils responding to a variety of sculptures and using the appropriate vocabulary. Anna notices that some of the pupils she rehearsed with are able to participate with the discussion and she is able to support some pupils by encouraging and reminding them.

Opportunities to use speaking and listening skills can also be provided through asking visitors into the classroom. Again preparation is necessary. Visitors should be briefed on what you are planning for the pupils to learn and the level of understanding of the pupils. Depending on the age and needs of the pupils, visitors might need to be aware of how long they can talk for and the sort of language they can use. It can be frustrating for teachers, pupils and visitors when there is a mismatch.

Speaking and listening around the school

Clearly there are many occasions when we can continue to develop pupils' speaking and learning skills informally in day-to-day school life. Sometimes it is only when we hear a child spontaneously and independently using exciting vocabulary, expressing an opinion articulately or reading aloud expressively in their class assembly that we realise that our teaching has been absorbed and is now part of the child's repertoire. Supporting children to develop social conversation with their peers and with adults is as important as using their speaking and listening skills in their work.

Exchanging greetings, initiating and maintaining conversation and having fun with words are vital to our social relationships and tend to contribute to a warm and positive classroom and school environment. As part of your role as a professional TA you will be aware of your role beyond the classroom you work in and the pupils you support. You will have encountered many opportunities to have fun with speaking and listening. These may include answering the register in different tones of voice, as story book characters and using different languages, sharing poetry and songs with the class, circle time activities and taking part in assemblies.

Summary

- The skills of speaking and listening, group discussion and interaction and drama are a significant component of the English curriculum and should be taught explicitly.
- They can be taught, used and applied through planned experiences in English or literacy lessons, across the curriculum and in day-to-day and real-life contexts.
- Your own speaking and listening provide a model for children's own skills.

References

Clipson-Boyles, S. (2001) *Supporting Language and Literacy 3 – 8*. London: David Fulton Publishers

Department for Education and Employment (1999) *The National Curriculum. Handbook for Primary Teachers in England*. London: DfEE

Department for Education and Skills (2003) *Speaking, Listening and Learning*. London: DfES

Department of Education and Skills (2005) *Speaking, Listening, Learning: Working with Children who have SEN*. London: DfES

Edwards, V. (1995) *Speaking and Listening in Multilingual Classrooms*. University of Reading: Reading and Language Information Centre

Goodwin, P. (2001) *The Articulate Classroom. Talking and Learning in the Primary School*. London: David Fulton Publishers

Grugeon, E., Hubbard, H., Smith, C. and Dawes, L. (eds) (2001) *Teaching Speaking and Listening in the Primary School*. London: David Fulton Publishers

Rose, R. (2005) *Becoming a Primary Higher Level Teaching Assistant*. Exeter: Learning Matters

4. Reading

Introduction

Learning to read is at the heart of primary learning and teaching and is the foundation for success in school. Being an enthusiastic and motivated reader who reads for pleasure and inspiration can have a positive impact on us all the way through our lives. When we engage in the teaching of reading we must consider not only acquisition of skills but also the promotion of positive attitudes to reading. From your experience in your own school and talking with colleagues from other schools you will be aware that schools approach the teaching of reading in a variety of ways. A recent Office for Standards in Education (Ofsted) report evaluating the teaching of reading in primary schools described key features of the successful teaching of reading (Ofsted 2005). These include some that have a direct impact on your role as a professional TA.

There is a great deal of research, guidance and resource material available to teachers to support their planning of reading experiences. It is likely that you have most recent DfES materials and guidance available to you in school, probably supplemented with published resources that your school has purchased.

In this chapter we will consider the range of strategies and ways of organising the teaching of reading in classrooms. We will focus on your role as a professional TA in shared, guided, independent and individual reading. We will address the range of skills that pupils need to develop to become successful and confident readers, such as decoding, understanding and responding to what they read. The role of parents and, in some schools, volunteers will be explored. Your relationship with parents and the other adults who support pupils' reading can ensure that pupils receive the sustained, specific and positive support that will help them make progress. The use of reading skills across the curriculum in purposeful contexts will be explored, including use of the school and local library. Your role in promoting pupils' love of reading and providing opportunities to give reading a high profile will be considered.

In particular, this chapter will focus on the standards in the box below.

HLTA STANDARDS

1.1   They have high expectations of all pupils; respect their social, cultural, linguistic, religious and ethnic backgrounds; and are committed to raising their educational achievement.

1.3   They demonstrate the positive values, attitudes and behaviour they expect from the pupils with whom they work.

1.4   They work collaboratively with colleagues, and carry out their roles effectively, knowing when to seek help and advice.

1.5   They are able to liaise sensitively and effectively with parents and carers, recognising their roles in pupils' learning.

3.1.1   They contribute effectively to teachers' planning and preparation of lessons.

3.1.2   Working within a framework set by the teacher, they plan their role in lessons including how they will provide feedback to pupils and colleagues on pupils' learning and behaviour.

3.1.3   They contribute effectively to the selection and preparation of teaching resources that meet the diversity of pupils' needs and interests.

3.3.1   Using clearly structured teaching and learning activities, they interest and motivate pupils, and advance their learning.

3.3.3   They promote and support the inclusion of all pupils in the learning activities in which they are involved.

3.3.6   They are able, where relevant, to guide the work of other adults supporting teaching and learning in the classroom.

CHAPTER OBJECTIVES

By the end of this chapter you should:

● have an understanding of the range of strategies and ways of organising the teaching of reading and reading skills that teachers use

● be aware of the significance of attitude and motivation on reading progress and consider ideas to develop and maintain enthusiasm for reading

● have an understanding of the ways in which parents and volunteers can be supported to support progress in reading

● have considered the range of situations and contexts in which pupils can use their reading skills purposefully

● know the importance of giving formative feedback to pupils and specific information to teachers when commenting on reading skills and progress.

Teaching strategies

From your experiences in school you will have observed teachers using a range of teaching strategies to support pupils' reading. How these strategies are combined and your role within them, will vary from school to school. It is likely that your understanding of each term will be related to how your school uses and adapts each strategy to fit its practice. The definitions below are taken from *Book Bands for Guided Reading* (Bickler and Baker 2003).

Shared reading

Shared reading takes place with the whole class in a mixed ability situation. The text is shared by using a big book, interactive whiteboard or overhead projector. The text is rich, challenging and likely to be beyond the current ability of most of the class. Pupils will be receiving a high level of support through explicit teaching, oral response and collaboration. The teacher will be introducing and practising planned objectives at word, sentence and text level.

Guided reading

Guided reading takes place with a small group of between three and eight pupils who are working at around the same level of reading. Ideally each pupil should have a text and the focus will be working on an unfamiliar text or section of text. The text will be at instructional level, allowing pupils to read and comprehend at/above 90 per cent accuracy. The teacher or TA will structure the task and then ask pupils to apply strategies that will have been introduced in shared reading. Pupils will be expected to read to themselves with the teacher or TA facilitating in order to reinforce and extend strategies and objectives.

Independent reading

Independent reading takes place individually or in small groups. Pupils will be reading a variety of texts from shared and guided reading and from the library. This range can also include reading games, activities, books on tape and environmental print such as instructions and recipes. The texts will be well within the capability of the pupils, allowing them to read and comprehend at/above 95 per cent accuracy. Pupils will work independently or with others to practise their reading in variety of contexts, or respond to their reading. The focus for independent reading will be for pupils to achieve fluency and flexibility at their current level and respond personally to the text.

(Adapted from Bickler and Baker 2003)

In addition to these teaching strategies many schools also include reading with individuals in their range of teaching. This may occur with all pupils or with identified pupils. As a professional TA this teaching activity may form a significant part of your role. Reading with individuals is a very time-intensive process and is therefore often prioritised according to the individual needs of pupils. Using the model above, individual reading can be defined as described below.

Individual reading

Individual reading will take place with one adult and one child. The length and frequency of reading sessions will vary from a few minutes to half an hour. The text will be at instructional level, allowing pupils to read and comprehend at/above 90 per cent accuracy. The support provided by the adult will be focused on personal learning objectives planned by the teacher in order to support progress in specific areas of reading. Providing specific developmental feedback and praise, encouraging independence and sustaining a positive attitude to reading will be crucial to supporting the pupil. Providing assessment information and notes in relation to the learning objectives for the teacher will help future planning.

Teachers and TAs may also use individual reading to check on pupils' progress, make assessments in order to adjust objectives or to investigate misconceptions.

PRACTICAL TASK

Consider the teaching strategies that you are involved in.

Compare them to the definitions above and note similarities and differences.

Consider your role in each type of teaching.

TEACHING STRATEGY	IN YOUR SCHOOL...	YOUR ROLE IN...
Shared reading		
Guided reading		
Independent reading		
Individual reading		

When you consider your role in each teaching strategy you might evaluate it in relation to the following points:

- Planning – do you follow teachers' planning or plan your own teaching?

- Teaching – do you support a teacher or take a lead role in teaching?

- Feedback – is your feedback to pupils and teachers related to learning objectives?

- Assessment – how to you communicate any assessment information?

- Resources – do you have a role in choosing, preparing and organising resources?

- Organisation – do you have a role in organising the class, groups or individuals in reading?

Developing the skills of reading

As a professional TA you will be aware of the range of strategies and skills pupils must learn and be able to apply in a balanced synthesis in order to be able to read successfully. Young children develop phonological awareness and learn to associate sounds with letters and groups of letters. They learn to read some words by sight. They use the clues available in pictures, the rhythm of language and their experience of life and stories. In the National Literacy Strategy the skills pupils need to learn in order to support successful reading are summarised in the visual image of the 'searchlights'.

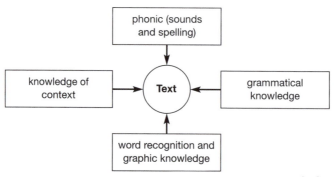

(DfEE 1998, p. 4)

SEARCHLIGHT CUE	DEFINITION	EXAMPLE
Phonics (sounds and spellings)	These cues are centred on the use of segmentation and blending of phonemes.	Segmenting a phonically regular word and blending the phonemes together to read a word 'b//e//n//ch.....bench' in the sentence 'He sat on the bench' confirmed by checking in the picture.
Grammatical knowledge	These cues are centred on using knowledge of how words fit together into sentences and using the cues available from punctuation.	Using the sentence structure to read the word 'into' in the sentence: 'The boy went *into* the playground' confirmed by using phonics and sight vocabulary.
Knowledge of context	These cues are centred on the literal and inferential information picked up from the text (characters, setting, plot, dialogue, text features) and from pictures.	Using the picture of the slide to read the word in the sentence: 'He went down the *slide*' confirmed by checking in the picture and using phonics.

Word recognition and graphic knowledge	These cues are centred on using sight vocabulary (initially from lists in the appendices of the NLS Framework) and the visual features of words and text.	Using sight vocabulary from List 1, Years 1 and 2 to read 'down' in the sentence: 'He went *down* the slide' confirmed by checking the picture and the sense of the sentence.

It is important that you know and understand how the range of reading skills fit together. It is likely that you will be supporting pupils to develop or strengthen specific aspects of their reading skills, possibly the aspects where they need additional support. You may be called upon to support pupils by prompting them to the searchlight cues. It is important that you choose the ones that will most successfully allow the pupil to decode the word, and be alert to pupils who rely too heavily on the same searchlight. It is also important to be aware of pupils' strengths, their ability to use several or all cues and give them feedback about what they are good at and doing right as well as where they need to improve. This will help maintain a positive attitude which is vital in developing lifelong readers. As a professional TA you should be looking to deliver the learning within a positive and motivating context. Ensuring that you introduce the learning effectively through preparing to read, or planning a book introduction, can support this process.

Preparing to read

Preparing to read, which in some plans is called the 'book introduction', can be carried out with individuals, groups or the whole class. What you plan to include in the book introduction will depend on factors such as where you are in the series of lessons, the length of the teaching session and how much prior learning you need the pupils to recall and reactivate. When planned and delivered effectively, this part of the teaching session can result in more success for the pupils and improved self-esteem. As Edwards (1995) suggests, familiarisation can be especially supportive for pupils who are learning English as an additional language. Planning this part of your lesson is crucial. When planning for shared reading you will consider the needs of the whole class; in guided reading you will be focused on the needs of your group; and in individual reading you will consider the individual and specific needs of the pupil you are working with. There are, however, some general factors that you may consider when planning your book introduction.

PRACTICAL TASK

Choose a book that you are using with pupils in shared, guided or individual reading.

Use the table below to consider some aspects you might include in your book introduction.

PROMPTS	NOTES ON YOUR TEXT
Is there anything you know from previous/ ongoing work with this class, group or individual that needs to be addressed?	
Are there any sight words, challenging words, character/place names that need to be introduced?	
Are there any phonemes that the class, group or individual are learning and could be revised before reading?	
Are there any searchlights or strategies that you need to remind pupils about?	
Is there anything about the context of the book that will be unfamiliar to the pupils?	
What prompts can you use to ensure pupils use and predict from the book cover?	
If you are continuing mid-story, what are the key aspects of the story that pupils will need to recall in order to continue reading?	
If you are using an information book, what features of the book will pupils need to know how to use?	

Depending on how long you have for your book introduction, it is likely that you will have to prioritise rather than include all of these points. It is important to consider the learning objectives of the entire lesson and identify which parts of the book introduction will be most supportive to the pupils' learning, consulting with the class teacher and using your professional judgement will help you in this. When you teach guided reading groups you will find that many published schemes include a book introduction or some useful information, such as key words or challenging vocabulary, that you can use as a book introduction in their planning notes. You might read some of these as a model for developing your own book introductions.

Decoding

At the early reading stage we are supporting pupils to use their skills to decode the texts they are reading. In doing this they are using their phonological knowledge to segment and blend phonemes, they are using any sight vocabulary that they know, they are predicting what words might or could come next from their experience of reading and what makes sense in English and they are using picture and context clues. On many occasions pupils are using more than one of these strategies and as their reading improves they are using combinations of these strategies rapidly as well as self-correcting where necessary. As teachers and TAs we teach these strategies, modelling them explicitly, giving positive and developmental feedback as pupils use them, choosing texts that allow pupils to learn and practise them at the appropriate level. It is also important that we allow pupils the time to try out, take risks, make mistakes and correct themselves. It can be agonising for adults to take this time, supply sensitive and appropriate prompts and make the decision about whether to wait or supply the word and move on.

Case study

Carrie is reading with Ali, a Year 1 pupil. They are reading a book called Presents *from the Heinemann Storyworlds set 'Our World Stage 5'. They have read another book from this set so Ali is familiar with the context, setting and the main characters.*

Grandma was on the garden bench.
She looked up at the blue sky.
It was like the blue sky in Pakistan.

Grandpa was in the house.
He looked out of the window.
He saw a red car.
'Uncle Sami and Raza are here,'
he said.

(Gavin, J. and James, R.N., 1996, Presents. *Oxford: Heinemann pages 2 and 3)*

Carrie is supporting Ali to help him use the searchlight strategies with more balance as she and the teacher have identified that he relies on picture and context clues more than phonics, grammatical knowledge and word recognition and graphic knowledge.

Carrie has made a visual prompt card to remind Ali of the range of strategies available to him in child-friendly language ('When I want to read a new word I...'). Before each reading session Carrie and Ali look at and talk about this.

When reading the double page shown above, Carrie has already thought through the appropriate prompts she can use if Ali needs support. She has tried to plan opportunities for Ali to use a combination of strategies or use one and confirm it by using another. Her thinking is shown below.

Phonics Context	Word recognition Phonics	Phonics Word recognition	Word recognition Grammatical knowledge	Phonics Context	Phonics Context
Grandma	**was**	**on**	**the**	**garden**	**bench.**

Word recognition Grammatical knowledge	Word recognition Phonics Context	Word recognition Phonics	Word recognition Grammatical knowledge	Word recognition Grammatical knowledge	Phonics Context	Context Phonics
She	**looked**	**up**	**at**	**the**	**blue**	**sky.**

Word recognition Phonics	Word recognition Phonics	Word recognition Grammatical knowledge	Word recognition Grammatical knowledge	Phonics Context	Context Phonics	Word recognition Phonics	Phonics Context
It	**was**	**like**	**the**	**blue**	**sky**	**in**	**Pakistan.**

Carrie knows she will not need to use all these prompts. Many of the words such as 'was', 'on', 'the', 'up', 'at', 'it', are part of Ali's sight vocabulary and she will encourage him to read these on sight without stopping to sound out each phoneme. She has identified Pakistan as the most potentially challenging word. In the conversation she plans to ask Ali if he remembers where grandpa and grandma used to live before they came to England. They talked about this when reading the previous book. This may be enough to help him read the word when it appears in the text. After reading, Carrie reviews the searchlights Ali has used with help and on his own, giving him and asking for examples so that he articulates his learning.

Learning and using phonic skills and grammatical knowledge will be covered further in Chapters 6 and 8.

Understanding and response

From even before children begin to learn to read independently they are responding to what we read to and with them and demonstrating their understanding by predicting, joining in, repeating, pointing and smiling. As children develop early reading skills, using their understanding to check for sense and meaning is an important strategy to them to learn to apply. As pupils achieve fluency and independence in reading, the focus of teaching and learning shifts to comprehension of and response to what they read. Teaching children to understand and engage with what they read will help them become enthusiastic and committed readers in the future.

Questioning during and after reading is a common strategy that teachers and TAs use to check pupils' understanding of what they read. In order to ensure that questioning is focused and effective we must consider the levels of questioning that will develop and deepen pupils' understanding. We can summarise these as follows.

Literal questions

The answers to literal questions are clear in the text. Literal questions tend to start with words such as 'who', 'when', 'where', 'what' or 'which'. We can support pupils to answer literal questions by making clear and explicit links between question words and likely answers; for example, if we are looking for the answer to a 'where' question we are looking for a place or setting. We can also encourage pupils to identify the words that tell us the answer in the text by underlining or highlighting and using the actual words within the answer. This can be modelled by TAs in shared, guided or individual reading and reading activities. Answering literal questions allows pupils to demonstrate that they have understood and recalled what they have read at a surface level.

Inferential or deductive questions

The answers to inferential or deductive questions are found by using a combination of clues. This is often expressed as 'reading between the lines'. We may also be called upon to use our common sense and experience to justify or explain reasons and motivations. These questions might start with 'why', ask pupils about word meanings, or character motivation and feelings. We can support pupils to answer these questions by modelling how we identify and combine clues to reach a reasonable answer. Answering inferential or deductive questions allows pupils to make connections, think more deeply and demonstrate that they have understood the wider implications of the text.

Response or evaluative questions

The answers to response or evaluative questions are found by considering how we feel about aspects of or the entire text, making connections with our experience and wider reading and justifying with reference to the text. These questions might ask for a justified opinion, an overview of the story theme or text type or comparison with other stories/texts. We can support pupils to answer these questions by modelling reasoned answers. We can ensure that we make links between pupils' reading going beyond the immediate text that we are concentrating on. We can also develop this aspect of comprehension through wider reading opportunities discussed later in this chapter.

As a professional TA it is likely that you will be planning the detail of the questioning you use with pupils after the teacher has indicated the general focus. Literacy lesson planning, planning for shared or guided reading or individual objectives may also identify a more specific focus such as answering a particular question type. If you bear in mind these three main question types and try to use a variety of questions from each, you will be able to maintain a balance and ensure that pupils are interacting with the text fully.

PRACTICAL TASK

Choose a text that you will be using with pupils.

Devise two questions of each question type.

Consider how you will support pupils to answer each question should they require scaffolding.

QUESTION TYPE	QUESTIONS	PROMPTS TO SCAFFOLD ANSWERS
Literal (clearly stated in the text)		
Inferential (interpretation that goes beyond the literal)		
Evaluative (meaning made by the reader)		

While questioning is a useful approach to check and develop understanding and response, there are many creative and imaginative strategies that can enrich your teaching repertoire when discussing texts with pupils. These include using clues to make and justify predictions, visualising characters, settings and plot events, and drama techniques such as hot-seating and role play. Pupils' responses in these more creative and imaginative situations can give you an insight into their understanding of characters' feelings and motives as well as being motivating for pupils.

By the time pupils are reading fluently, independently and silently, the use of a reading journal, diary or log can help you to structure pupils' responses, research and independent reading. Carefully planned reading diary tasks can help to initiate shared discussion about pupils' reading, motivating them to read further. Tasks can also be tied into word, sentence and text-level objectives or individual learning targets.

Case study

Tom is a TA in a Year 4 classroom. He monitors the reading of eight fluent and independent readers. The group consists of five boys and three girls. The class teacher has identified that they are reading at above a stage appropriate for their ages, but is keen to develop their enthusiasm for reading with a focus on sharing their ideas, responses and understanding. The pupils already record basic information about what they read in a reading log. Tom is going to use this log as a vehicle for setting tasks and challenges for the group to pursue independently and then share as a group once a week. Tom introduces the idea to the group using some books from the Year 4 Term 2 range of 'stories/novels about imagined worlds'. He initiates a discussion by asking the pupils to look through a variety of stories and novels and identify those which are set in 'imagined worlds' and say more about their decisions. The pupils use illustrations, covers, the blurb and reading the first page or two to sort the books, beginning to define the term more clearly as they talk. Tom then sets the next challenge for the group. Reading the first chapter of the story 'Coraline' by Neil Gaiman, he asks them to make a prediction about the imagined world Coraline will enter, justifying their choice from their reading. The discussion at the next session is lively as there are several possibilities – the well, the bricked-up door, the circus mice and the garden. In subsequent sessions the group are encouraged to think more deeply about this focus text and read independently within the same genre and make connections. Tom structures the reading log tasks to address reading objectives, sustain interest and develop group interaction skills. This involves Tom in a certain amount of reading of his own, in order to keep up with the group and set relevant tasks.

In the case study outlined above Tom has a clear idea of the teacher's aims for the pupils' reading as a group and in relation to literacy lessons. He is given the freedom to adjust his teaching to support another key priority for the teacher, sustaining a positive attitude to reading. His creative use of the reading log lifts it from being a mere record of what was read. In the future these activities might be extended by making a link to television and film adaptations, making contact with other readers through email, and researching authors. Tom is contributing to creating what Goodwin (1999) refers to as a community of readers, who spark ideas through purposeful discussion.

Using reading skills across the curriculum

As well as reading fiction and poetry, it is important for pupils to learn and use the skills that support reading for information across a range of curriculum subjects and interests. The skills necessary to access information texts must be planned and taught in meaningful contexts and purposeful activities. These include identifying and being able to use the distinctive features of information texts such as the contents, index, glossary, headings and subheadings, illustrations, tables and other graphic conventions. The skills of skimming – looking over a text quickly to locate a key word – and scanning – reading to gain an overview of the passage – must also be taught explicitly.

Wray and Lewis (1997) suggest that while many pupils can perform these skills in isolation, they find choosing the appropriate strategy and applying it effectively and at the appropriate time more challenging. There is scope for the professional TA to help pupils to use their information retrieval across all areas of the curriculum. As teachers aim to make more explicit links between literacy and other areas of the curriculum this may become more apparent in primary classrooms.

Attitudes to reading

As a professional TA you will already be aware of the significance of high self-esteem, having a positive attitude and being willing to take risks to successful learning. This is especially true in learning to read and becoming a lifelong reader. Research has shown that being more enthusiastic about reading and being a frequent reader is more of an advantage, on its own, than having well-educated parents in good jobs (OECD 2000). There are many ways in which you can make a contribution to developing and sustaining a positive attitude to reading in school and beyond the school. You can ensure that you are a good role model, seen reading, being enthusiastic about reading at every opportunity.

The choices we make about which resources to use in teaching and learning experiences play an important role in inspiring and including pupils. Bringing stories to life with story sacks can be an exciting way in for younger children. The parallel non-fiction resource 'curiosity kits' can also be motivating, especially when tailored to meet children's interests. Using bilingual texts and CD-ROMs can support bilingual pupils and alert all pupils to the range of languages spoken and read in our schools. As a professional TA you should also be aware of addressing stereotyping and cultural diversity through imaginative and sensitive choice of resources. You can use your choice of reading resources to widen pupils' experiences and confirm that their own lives and families appear in stories. Taking time to evaluate the texts you are using so you can match them to pupils' interests, learning needs and familiar experiences can have a significant impact on pupils' engagement with reading.

The school library can be a valuable resource and source of inspiration and excitement about reading. If your role is focused on supporting English, taking a lead role in developing the school library to meet the needs of the pupils, staff and parents can underpin a vibrant English curriculum. Ensuring that books are well organised and attractively presented is important. Making links to authors, shadowing book prizes, and linking books to film and television can place reading firmly into real life. Participating in local and national book events such as World Book Day and National Poetry Day can be fun for children. Making links with your local library and encouraging pupils and families to use local resources effectively can enable pupils to get into good study habits for the future and maintain their reading through longer holidays. Local libraries are usually keen to make links with schools and can be a valuable source of ideas, resources and access to events.

Working with parents and volunteers

Schools vary in their approach to individual reading both in school and at home. Many schools make the most of the enthusiasm of parents of younger children to support their children's progress at home. As Graham and Kelly (1997) suggest, parents are potentially in the very best position to make reading a personally rich and rewarding experience for children. At best, schools can involve parents actively in reading with their children through specific initiatives (Ofsted 2005). For parental involvement in reading to be effective it must be underpinned by good communication between parents and school staff, good-quality resources that are well matched to the learning needs and interests of pupils and appropriate training opportunities for parents.

In your role as a professional TA you may be involved in some aspects of home school reading. You may be best placed to support parents with their children's reading, especially if you are supporting individual pupils in school as well. You will know from your experience that teaching pupils to read can be challenging for teachers and TAs. It is important to keep this in mind when you ask parents to become partners in this process. Short, regular conversations with parents about what the child is learning, how best to support the child in applying reading skills and positive feedback about what the child is doing well can help to sustain parental interest and involvement. You can also communicate through a written reading diary if this is more appropriate to the needs of the parent.

Case study

Kerry is a TA working in a Year 1 classroom. She has taken responsibility for the reading of six pupils who are working at around the same level. She plans and teaches guided reading sessions with the group and reads with them individually from time to time to monitor their progress. The pupils take home a book to read at home on a regular basis. Kerry is aware that with frequent and focused practice the pupils will make better progress but finding the time to address this within the school day is a challenge. Kerry discusses this concern with the class teacher and suggests that she talk with the children's parents with a view to involving them in reading with the children at home in a focused way that will back up the learning taking place at school. With the support of the class teacher Kerry contacts the parents to find out how interested they would be and arranges to see them together to talk further. At the first meeting Kerry talks to the parents about what she is doing with the pupils at school, focusing on using the searchlights and segmenting and blending phonemes. With the help of another TA she role-plays the prompts, questions and praise that she is using with the pupils. After this session Kerry plans to be available as the parents drop off their children at school and as they collect them from school once a week so they can ask her any questions and she can update them about the children's reading in school. The parents can also use the daily reading diary to communicate with Kerry about the home reading. Over time Kerry develops positive relationships with the parents, some of whom prefer face-to-face support; some prefer to use the reading diary. It is clear from the pupils' progress that the focused support at home is having an impact. After about six weeks Kerry meets with the parents again to celebrate the pupils' progress and thanks them for their part in it. She also shares with them the next steps for the children, shows them how to adapt their support and answers questions. The parents also appear to enjoy sharing their experiences.

In the case study presented above the role of the professional TA transforms the pupils' home reading from a general and rather unfocused experience to an experience that is supportive to what the pupils are learning in school. Her input and relationship with the parents ensures that the parents have someone to check with, ask questions of and share how the reading is going. They also understand the importance of their role in the partnership. This results in parents being more committed to and enthusiastic about reading with the children. Many schools actively involve their parents in supporting their children's reading in a focused and organised way. Short training sessions can ensure parents understand how to support effectively, as can written information such as leaflets and reading diaries. This support and communication is especially important as pupils become more fluent readers and the support required moves towards understanding and response.

Other schools address individual reading by using volunteers who again must be trained, supported and updated. The professional TA can play a lead role in developing these partnerships.

Summary

Effective support for reading includes:

- planning a range of purposeful, motivating and exciting opportunities in which to read
- using the range of searchlight strategies in decoding
- using a well-planned range questions to elicit response and develop understanding
- giving positive and development feedback that will lead to improvement
- involving parents in reading with children at home.

References

Bickler, S. and Baker, S. (2003) *Book Bands for Guided Reading* (third edition). London: University of London Insititute of Education

Department for Education and Employment (1998). *The National Literacy Strategy Framework for Teaching*. London: DfEE

Edwards, V. (1995) *Reading in Multilingual Classrooms*. University of Reading: Reading and Language Information Centre

Gaiman, N. (2002) *Coraline*. London: Bloomsbury

Gavin, J. and James, R.N. (1996) *Presents*. Oxford: Heinemann

Goodwin, P. (ed.) (1999) *The Literate Classroom*. London: David Fulton Publishers Ltd

Graham, J. and Kelly, A. (1998) *Reading Under Control*. London: David Fulton Publishers Ltd

Ofsted (2005) *Reading for Purpose and Pleasure. An Evaluation of the Teaching of Reading in Primary Schools*. London: Ofsted

Organisation for Economic Co-operation and Development (2000) *Reading for Change*. Paris: OECD

Programme for International Student Assessment. In Foster, A. (2003) Making International Comparisons. *Literacy Today*, issue 36

Wray, D. and Lewis, M. (1997) *Extending Literacy – Children Reading and Writing Non-Fiction*. London: Routledge

5. Writing

Introduction

There is no doubt that learning to write is a challenging undertaking. It is likely that you are called upon to write in your role as a professional TA. Perhaps you contribute reports for reviews, write plans, and supply written feedback to teachers and parents. You may currently be writing your HLTA tasks. Each of these forms of writing requires us to consider the audience, the purpose, the content, the vocabulary and the structure of the writing. You may be modifying these almost instinctively if they are very familiar forms of writing to you, or you may have to research by looking at models, drafting, talking with others and improving your work before you feel it is appropriate for the intended audience and purpose. Reflecting upon this process will help you to empathise with the feelings of the pupils you support and teach who are at the early stages of this process and may have less experience from which to draw.

The teaching of writing and how we equip pupils with the skills they need to be effective and successful writers is an issue under constant scrutiny. It is a complex process which may require pupils to draw upon ideas, information, thoughts and feelings. At the same time they must make decisions about the words they will use, how to spell them and ensure they are legible, and they must consider how they will fit words together into sentences and how these will be structured, punctuated and presented. As Graham and Kelly (1998) suggest, there is a useful distinction to be made between the two aspects of writing: composition and transcription. In this chapter the focus will be on composition. The teaching and learning of writing must be underpinned by and linked to the teaching and learning of speaking, listening and reading. Writing must be used in purposeful and motivating contexts, and inspired by real experiences and events. It is important that you can see this bigger picture, although you may be called upon to support pupils in specific aspects on a day-to-day basis.

In this chapter we will consider the range of strategies and ways of organising the teaching of writing in classrooms. We will focus on your role as a professional TA in shared, guided and independent writing. This will include considering the features of the different types of writing that pupils need to learn. We will address the range of skills that pupils need to develop to become successful and confident writers and how we might support them in moving towards becoming more independent writers. Your role in supplying positive and formative feedback to pupils to help them make improvements to their writing will be explored. The use of writing skills across the curriculum in purposeful contexts will be explored. Your role in promoting a positive attitude towards writing and providing opportunities to give writing a high profile will be considered. Transcriptional aspects of writing such as handwriting, spelling, grammar and punctuation will be considered in more depth in subsequent chapters.

In particular, this chapter will focus on the standards in the box below.

HLTA STANDARDS

1.2 They build and maintain successful relationships with pupils, treating them consistently, with respect and consideration, and are concerned for their development as learners.

1.6 They are able to improve their own practice, including through observation, evaluation and discussion with colleagues.

2.1 They have sufficient understanding of their specialist area to support pupils' learning, and are able to acquire further knowledge to contribute effectively and with confidence to the classes in which they are involved.

2.5 They know the key factors that can affect the way pupils learn.

3.1.1 They contribute effectively to teachers' planning and preparation of lessons.

3.1.2 Working within a framework set by the teacher, they plan their role in lessons including how they will provide feedback to pupils and colleagues on pupils' learning and behaviour.

3.1.3 They contribute effectively to the selection and preparation of teaching resources that meet the diversity of pupils' needs and interests.

3.3.1 Using clearly structured teaching and learning activities, they interest and motivate pupils, and advance their learning.

3.3.2 They communicate effectively and sensitively with pupils to support their learning.

3.3.3 They promote and support the inclusion of all pupils in the learning activities in which they are involved.

3.3.5 They advance pupils' learning in a range of classroom settings, including working with individuals, small groups and whole classes where the assigned teacher is not present.

By the end of this chapter you should:

- have developed an understanding of the range of strategies and ways of organising the teaching of writing and writing skills that teachers use

- be aware of the significance of attitude and motivation on writing progress and have considered ideas to develop and maintain enthusiasm for writing

- have considered the range of situations and contexts in which pupils can use their writing skills purposefully

- know the importance of giving formative feedback to pupils and specific information to teachers when commenting on writing skills and progress.

Creating a supportive classroom for writing

As a professional TA you have probably worked with pupils who are reluctant to write, who feel uncertain about their writing, indeed you may have felt this way yourself. Pupils may be anxious about committing their ideas to paper, find it hard to juggle all the skills required to write and can be easily deflected. Creating a supportive learning environment for writing is essential to developing a positive attitude towards writing for all children.

Your role may be focused upon groups and individuals who find writing challenging. Creating a positive attitude is all the more crucial for pupils who may find writing additionally challenging, such as boys, pupils learning English as an additional language and pupils with special educational needs. Some of the resources and strategies you put into place to support groups of pupils with specific needs may well support all children. These include:

- ensuring that pupils have the opportunity to rehearse their writing orally, 'talking before writing' in a planned and purposeful way with adults or with each other

- giving pupils the chance to recall prior learning

- ensuring that writing tasks and planned outcomes have an audience and purpose, preferably beyond the adults and children in the classroom

- using high-quality, motivating resources including ICT, films and TV, multi-modal texts, etc.

- taking learning styles into account and including a range of visual, auditory and kinaesthetic activities

- matching instructions and teaching to the pupils' ability to understand and remember them and providing prompts to help them recall them

- being clear when giving feedback in relation to the lesson objective rather than talking about the whole piece of writing and all the errors in it

- providing scaffolds to the transcription aspect of writing including picture/word prompts, acting as scribe, using ICT
- working from a clear and shared learning objective with specific success criteria all expressed in language of the appropriate level for the pupils
- praising effort, risk-taking and perseverance.

Before writing

Before we ask pupils to write, it is important that we plan experiences in speaking and listening and reading that will support their writing. If your school uses the NLS unit plan as the basis for sequences of teaching you will be familiar with making explicit links between pupils' reading and their writing. Over a period of about two weeks the sequence of work follows this pattern:

Reading

Pupils read and respond to a text type. The teacher demonstrates strategies, pupils practise them.

Analysis

Pupils explore text structure and language features of the text type. They explore the principles of effective writing that relates to the text types.

Writing

The teacher demonstrates supported writing so pupils develop the confidence to do it independently. Pupils apply the principles they have learned to create their own writing.

(*The Literacy Planning CD-ROM*, DfES 2004)

This sequence, starting with good-quality, well-chosen texts, and moving to the pupils' own writing, provides a clear model to scaffold their own writing. It has implications for your teaching since it will be important that you are clear about the elements from the reading you will be asking pupils to use in their writing. Looking at the whole sequence of the unit plan, and in particular the objectives, will help you understand these links and allow you to support pupils effectively.

In the case study overleaf, access to planning in advance of the teaching is crucial to Alice's ability to fulfil her role as a professional TA. Since beginning to anticipate in this way, Alice has felt better prepared in terms of her subject knowledge and has been able to address any gaps that are apparent. She has also been able to ensure she is prepared for the role she will play and has sufficient time to adapt teaching resources to meet the needs of the pupils she will support. In particular, she has been able to ensure that she explicitly teaches features of text when reading that she can see pupils will need in their writing.

Case study

Alice is a TA working with a Year 4 class. The next unit of work is based on The Julian Stories by Ann Cameron. The focus for the unit is developing character and setting. Text-level objectives from Y4 Term 1 include:

T1 to investigate how settings and characters are built up from small details, and how the reader responds to them
T2 to identify the main characteristics of the key characters, drawing on the text to justify views and using the information to predict actions
T11 write character sketches, focusing on small details to evoke sympathy or dislike.

Alice is able to make her own copy of the unit plan so that she can look ahead at the links between reading and writing across the sequence of teaching. She ensures that she reads the texts that will be used and annotates them with questions, teaching points and issues to follow up relating to the objectives she will be working from. Alice has clear idea of the small details that the author, Ann Cameron, uses to develop characters and describe the settings in the stories she will be using with the pupils. She is clear about how analysis of the text and teaching activities will scaffold pupils' writing, leading to an outcome where they try to include small details of character description in their own writing. Alice is able to anticipate some of the challenges the group she usually works with will face. She adapts some of the teaching resources and activities to meet their individual needs, for example by including some additional speaking and listening activities and making a collection of vocabulary that will help her group when they write.

Teaching strategies

Since the introduction of the National Literacy Strategy, a number of strategies to support the teaching of writing have been promoted through training and guidance materials. Schools tend to draw upon the range of strategies within their overall structure for the teaching of writing, adapting them to meet the needs of their pupils. If you look closely at the unit plan or the plan for a sequence of lessons, it is likely that you will see some or all of these strategies used at different points of the teaching sequence.

Shared writing

In shared writing the pupils will be focused on the teacher. The teacher will be working with the whole class. In shared writing the teacher will be choosing from the following models for teaching.

Demonstration

The teacher demonstrates the writing in relation to an objective and specific teaching points. The teacher makes decisions and thinks aloud as she has ideas, changes them and re-reads them. The pupils watch and listen.

Teacher scribing

The teacher takes ideas from the pupils and discusses and refines them in relation to the objective and teaching points. The pupils talk with each other, make suggestions, responding to the teacher's prompts and questions. The teacher tries to ensure that as many pupils as possible join in.

Supported composition

The teacher encourages the pupils to have a go, asking them to write directly related to the demonstration or shared writing. The pupils work with little whiteboards, possibly in pairs, contributing their ideas and outcomes.

It is useful for you to observe the teaching strategies the teacher uses so that you can use them when teaching. Following this whole-class direct teaching, teachers will also be planning opportunities for pupils to write for themselves. This involves guided writing and independent writing.

Guided writing

In guided writing the pupils will be organised in a group. The group will be composed of pupils working at around the same level, or with particular needs or targets in common. The teacher or TA will be teaching at the point of writing, giving immediate formative feedback and modelling in relation to the targets or objectives.

Independent writing

In independent writing pupils are given the opportunity to put what they are learning about writing into practice for themselves.

Developing the skills of writing

You will be using the teaching strategies that the class teacher models and plans, to ensure that the pupils receive consistent guidance and prompts. It is important that you use the strategies teachers are using so that you are not out of step with the school policy. Having the opportunity to observe a teacher working with a group in shared or guided writing can allow you to develop your own teaching strategies. Being observed by a teacher can also provide you with valuable feedback about your work.

PRACTICAL TASK

Over a unit or sequence of linked lessons make notes about the teaching strategies you observe and your own role in them.

TEACHING STRATEGY	EXAMPLES IN MY CLASSROOM	MY ROLE IN...
Shared writing – demonstration		
Shared writing – teacher scribing		
Shared writing – supported composition		
Guided writing		
Independent writing		

Consider your role in relation to these questions:

- Is it clear on the planning what your role is?

- Are there any questions you can discuss with the teacher in order to clarify or improve your role?

- Are there any areas where you need to improve your own subject knowledge in order to fulfil your role effectively?

- Are there any strategies that you have observed the teacher using that you can integrate into your own teaching?

You will also be choosing teaching strategies and adapting them in response to the individual needs of the groups and individuals you work with. You may get some insight from individual education plans (IEPs), other support plans such as those for pupils learning English as an additional language and training on support strategies to meet the needs of pupils with special educational needs.

Some of the generic teaching skills you might be expected to have in your repertoire have been outlined in the First Steps materials (Dewsbury and Bindon 1999). These include:

- helping pupils to rehearse sentences orally before writing them down
- encouraging the automatic habit of incorporating basic elements such as capital letters, full stops
- constantly and cumulatively re-reading and asking pupils to reread to assess coherence and flow
- calling upon pupils to explain why choices have been made, and decisions taken
- checking for misconceptions and dealing with them through discussion
- occasionally making deliberate errors to allow pupils to identify and correct them
- modelling metalanguage – the language used to talk about writing
- demonstrating how particular grammatical features are important/useful in context.

In the case study below, Janet has a clear idea of the entire sequence of lessons, how the learning connects together and what the specific learning objective for this lesson is. She is able to give positive and formative feedback in the form promoted by the school policy, highlighting where Tabir has met the learning objective and supporting him to make an improvement to his work. Although it is clear there are other improvements to be made, Janet maintains her focus on the lesson objective which is appropriate to the plan she is working from. She notes other errors to discuss with the teacher, such as Tabir and some of the other pupils' use of 't' instead 'ed' at the end of past-tense words. This will allow the teacher to incorporate this into future sentence-level teaching for the class.

Case study

Janet is a TA working with a group of Year 2 pupils. The class she is working with are working on a unit related to narrative in Year 2 Term 1 based on the story Dogger *by Shirley Hughes. Towards the end of the unit the pupils were telling stories of when they had lost something. This has given them the opportunity to rehearse their ideas orally and gain some feedback about the structure of the story. In this lesson the pupils go on to write their own story independently. The learning objective is to use the language of time to structure their story.*

Janet reminds the pupils of previous learning – they have identified time connectives in their reading, made collections of time connectives and tried to use them in their storytelling. Janet has made a list of common time connectives to support the group. As they write, Janet helps them re-read their writing and articulate decisions, and she reminds them of the learning objective.

Using a highlighter, Janet helps Tabir identify where he has met the learning objective. He has used 'last week' and 'then' in his writing.

To help him improve his work in relation to the learning objective she asks him to tell her more about when the dog came along. She indicates this with an arrow. He explains how the dog appears quite suddenly having run far from its owner. Janet suggests that an additional sentence starting with the word 'suddenly' would be a good improvement.

Tabir adds this to his writing below. Janet also notes that he (and several other pupils) need reminding about 'ed' at the end of past-tense words. She will discuss this with the class teacher.

Lst week I lost my football in the pick. I felt vry mad.

A dog busted my secked ball and the dog chast me. the dog ran away. Then I got my ball and I bumpt it up. I felt happy.

Tabir Y2

Last week I lost my football in the park. I felt very mad. A dog burst my second ball and the dog chased me the dog ran away. Then I got my ball and I pumped it up. I felt happy.

Suddenly a dog appeared.

Writing fiction, poetry and non-fiction

The range of fiction, poetry and non-fiction that pupils will encounter is specified in the NLS for each term. Teachers then make choices of texts that will allow them to make strong and explicit connections between reading and writing. It is important that you understand the main features of the texts you are using. You might consider the purpose, audience, and text, sentence and word-level features specific to the text type. This will help you support pupils' writing more effectively. You can develop this knowledge through your own reading. It is likely that you have access to many recent DfES publications, or you can access them online. The publications outlined below are a starting point.

Fiction

You can use the following publications to develop your knowledge of the main features of writing fiction:

Writing Fliers

Some of these discuss fiction aspects of writing such as narrative and play scripts. These provide some basic information.

Developing Early Writing

On pp. 152–3 there is a summary of the organisation and language features of fiction at Key Stage 1.

Grammar for Writing

On pp. 152–153 there is a summary of the organisation and language features of fiction at Key Stage 2.

Aspects of Narrative

These outline the relevant termly objectives in Key Stages 1 and 2, writing explanations and principles, and either:

- themes, structure and organisation, setting, characterisation and style

or

- annotated examples, key teaching ideas and key points for young writers/storytellers.

Poetry

You can use the following publications to develop your knowledge of strategies for teaching and learning the writing of poetry:

Writing Fliers

One of these discusses poetry. It provides some basic information.

Developing Early Writing

On pp. 152–3 there is a summary of the organisation and language features of poetry at Key Stage 1.

Grammar for Writing

On p. 152–3 there is a summary of the organisation and language features of poetry at Key Stage 2.

Non-fiction

As with fiction, the range of non-fiction text types is specified in the NLS. These include: recount, on-chronological report, instructions, explanation, persuasion and discussion.

You can use the following publications to develop your knowledge of the main features of writing non-fiction:

Writing Fliers

There is one for each of the six non-fiction text types listed above. These provide some basic information.

Developing Early Writing

On pp. 154–5 there is a summary of the organisation and language features of non-fiction text types at Key Stage 1.

Grammar for Writing

On pp. 154–5 there is a summary of the organisation and language features of non-fiction text types at Key Stage 2.

Non-fiction Strand Tracker

The non-fiction strand trackers take each text type and list all the termly objectives from Year R to Year 6 as they appear in the NLS. Each text type is followed by a list of relevant DfES resources and publications. Also included are strand trackers for using dictionaries and other alphabetical texts, non-fiction skills, locating information, note-making, organisational features, recording information and critical literacy.

Using writing skills across the curriculum

As discussed in earlier chapters, it is essential to make strong connections between what pupils read and what they write. When we are working on non-fiction writing there are many contexts in which text types can be used in a purposeful way in other areas of the curriculum. Clearly if pupils are writing an explanation or a report they need a context and sufficient background knowledge from which to write. Opportunities for these links are most effectively made at the long- or medium-term planning stage.

Ensuring that pupils have enough experience of reading and writing in non-fiction text types is essential if pupils are going to understand the main features such as vocabulary, connectives and structure (Wray and Lewis 1999). As with writing fiction, choosing an appropriate text and explicitly examining the key features supports effective writing in the chosen form.

In the case study opposite the TA has a clear idea of the text type and the objectives for the unit of work. As the unit progresses he identifies areas where he can provide additional support such as by providing picture and word prompts, using ICT and speaking and listening to support pupils' writing. Working with the teacher, he is able to support pupils' writing in an exciting and motivating context. He finds that pupils want to write for the audience of their friends in the next classroom and this spurs them on to write for a real audience and use the text type effectively. The results of their success are apparent for everyone to see when the decorations are put up for the Christmas party.

Case study

Jack is a TA working with a Year 2 class. The class are working on instructions in Year 2 Term 1. The literacy objectives are:

Reading comprehension
T13 to read simple instructions in the classroom, simple recipes, plans, instructions for constructing something.
T14 to note key structural features, e.g. clear statement of purpose at the start, sequential steps set out in a list, direct language.

Writing composition
T15 to write simple instructions, e.g. getting to school, playing a game.
T16 to use models from reading to organise instructions sequentially, e.g. listing points in order, each point depending on the previous one, numbering.
T18 to use appropriate register in writing instructions, i.e. direct, impersonal, building on texts read.
(DfEE 1998, p. 27)

In addition to this the unit of work has links to DT where pupils are:
Developing, planning and communicating ideas
Working with tools, equipment, materials and components to make quality products.

At the start of the unit of work the pupils read a set of instructions from the Big Book Fun Things to Make and Do *(Casseldon 1997) and several other sets of instructions made by Jack and the class teacher following the same model. As the pupils read and follow these sets of instructions the focus is on the key features of the instructions and how these help the pupils make items such as a puzzle, a necklace, and a greetings card. Jack uses the unit objectives to focus pupils how the clear title, numbered steps and specific language make it easier for them to produce the item. It also becomes clear that in this type of instruction a section called 'You will need...', which allows pupils to list tools, equipment and materials is very useful. As the pupils work, Jack makes a picture and word list of some common tools, equipment and materials to support some pupils in their reading and later writing. He also makes some jigsaws of familiar instructions for pupils to complete to focus them on the layout and sequence of the form. As the pupils move from reading and analysis to their own writing, the teacher helps the class write a set of prompts that they will use as criteria for writing and evaluating their own instructions. Towards the end of the unit of work the pupils work in groups to devise instructions for each other to make different types of Christmas decoration. Jack supports some of them in using the digital camera to make picture prompts. The test of their instructions is to swap with the parallel class, make the decorations and evaluate their effectiveness using the criteria they put together earlier. Jack is impressed by the level of motivation and determination to devise clear instructions. He encourages pupils to practise their instructions on each other to arrive at the clearest way of expressing their intentions.*

Choose a fiction text/texts that a unit of work is based on.

Use the chart below to identify and analyse the features.

	TEXT TYPE	TITLE: AUTHOR:
	Consider the general features of the text type	Look for examples in the text to use in reading and writing activities
Purpose What is the writing for? Audience Who is the writing for? Text features Structure, layout Sentence features Word features Specific vocabulary		

If you use published resources, the teachers' guide and other support material may have information to support you.

Scaffolding writing using story plans and writing frames

It is likely that when you are called upon to support pupils' writing you may use plans and writing frames to scaffold pupils' work and provide a supportive framework. Although there are many published versions of these available, if you to are provide the specific support that pupils need these must be evaluated carefully and often require adapting to be most effective. As Wray and Lewis (1997) point out, writing frames must not become formulaic or be used as 'writing worksheets' that are an end in themselves. As a professional TA you might be involved in designing, adapting and using plans and frames to support the writing of individuals, groups and the class. When you are designing a plan or writing frame you should ensure that you work from the shared reading and shared writing experiences and model, devising and using the frame flexibly.

To follow up the example in the case study on page 63, the TA could devise the following writing frame to support instruction writing:

This generic framework for instructions to make an item includes space for:

- a title 'How to make a...'
- a list of materials, tools and equipment 'You will need...'
- a box for each step, numbered in order.

It can be modified to support individuals by:

- including prompts such as 'How to...', 'You will need...'
- including numbers to remind pupils of the step-by-step nature of the instructions
- adding more boxes for longer sequences of instructions
- adding lines to guide writing
- adding a picture/photo prompt to each instruction box.

Summary

Effective support of writing includes:

- understanding the features of the genres of writing
- contributing to a positive environment where pupils are encouraged to take risks and make improvements
- planning a range of purposeful, motivating and exciting opportunities to inspire writing
- using your awareness of the range of teaching skills and strategies to scaffold learning
- giving positive and development feedback that will lead to improvement.

References

Bindon, R. (1999) *Shared and Guided Reading and Writing 2*. Oxford: Ginn Heinemann

Cameron, A. (1982) *The Julian Stories*. London: Fontana

Casseldon, R. (1997) *Fun Things to Make and Do*. Oxford: Heinemann Educational Publishers

Dewsbury, A. and Bindon, R. (1999) *Shared and Guided Reading and Writing 1*. Oxford: Ginn Heinemann

DfES *Aspects of Narrative*
Available from www.standards.gov.uk *under 'teaching resources'*

Casseldon, R. (1997) *Fun Things to Make a Do*. Oxford: Heinemann Educational Publishers

Department for Education and Employment (1998) *The National Literacy Strategy Framework for Teaching*. London: DfEE

Department for Education and Skills (2001) *Developing Early Writing*. London: DfES

Department for Education and Skills (2001) *Writing Fliers*. London: DfES

Department for Education and Employment (2000) *Grammar for Writing*. London: DfEE

Department for Education and Skills (2004) *The Literacy Planning CD-ROM*. London: DfES

Graham, J. and Kelly, A. (1998) *Writing Under Control*. London: David Fulton

Wray, D. and Lewis, M. (1997) *Extending Literacy. Children Reading and Writing Non-Fiction*. London: Routledge

Wray, D. and Lewis, M (1999) *The Problems and Possibilities of Non-Fiction Writing*. In Goodwin, P (ed) (1999) The Literate Classroom. London: David Fulton

6. Phonological awareness and phonics

Introduction

Research has shown that 'children's awareness of the phonemic structure of spoken words is a strong indicator of future success in learning to read' (Graham and Kelly 1997, p. 12). Over the last year there has been considerable discussion about the teaching of phonics. You may have seen research and comment in national newspapers and on television, and talked about it with colleagues in the staffroom. It may already have had an impact on thinking and practice in your school. It will be important for you, as a professional TA, to remain alert to the most recent research, guidance and resources and the implications they have for your teaching.

For many TAs, especially those working in literacy and English lessons, supporting pupils with phonics in reading and writing is a key aspect of the role. You may be delivering catch-up programmes with small groups of pupils, as well as supporting them in the classroom to ensure they transfer the knowledge, skills and understanding from your sessions into their work with the whole class. You may have received some specific training in this area related to the type of catch-up programme or published resources that your school uses. It is important for you to be able to connect this with your overall understanding of how children learn to speak, listen, read and write.

In this chapter we will consider what phonics is and how it is used in the development of reading. (Using phonics in spelling will be considered in a later chapter.) You will be encouraged to audit and extend your own subject knowledge in relation to phonics to ensure that you can support at levels appropriate to the pupils you work with. Developmental stages and age-related expectations will also be considered. We will explore the strategies that teachers and TAs use to teach phonics, including use of catch-up programmes. In particular, this chapter will focus upon the standards highlighted in the box below:

HLTA STANDARDS

1.1 They have high expectations of all pupils; respect their social, cultural, linguistic, religious and ethnic backgrounds; and are committed to raising their educational achievement.

1.2 They demonstrate and promote the positive values, attitudes and behaviour they expect from pupils with whom they work.

1.5 They are able to liaise sensitively and effectively with parents and carers, recognising their roles in pupil's learning.

▶

2.1　They have sufficient understanding of their specialist area to support pupil's learning, and are able to acquire further knowledge to contribute effectively and with confidence to the classes in which they are involved.

2.2　They are familiar with the school curriculum, the age-related expectations of pupils, the main teaching methods and the testing/examination frameworks in the subjects and age ranges in which they are involved.

2.3　They understand the aims, content, teaching strategies and intended outcomes for the lesson in which they are involved, and understand the place of these in the related teaching programme.

3.1.1　They contribute effectively to teachers' planning and preparation of lessons.

3.1.2　Working within a framework set by the teacher, they plan their role in lessons including how they will provide feedback to pupils and colleagues on pupil's learning and behaviour.

3.3.1　Using clearly structured teaching and learning activities, they interest and motivate pupils, and advance their learning.

3.3.5　They advance pupil's learning in a range of classroom settings, including working with individuals, small groups and whole classes where the assigned teacher is not present.

CHAPTER OBJECTIVES

By the end of this chapter you should:

- know more about what phonics is and some of the current research about phonics teaching

- be aware of the developmental stages and age-related expectations in the teaching of phonological awareness and phonics

- have developed an understanding of the range of strategies for the teaching of phonic skills that teachers use

- be aware of the range of catch-up programmes and your role in working with these

- have considered your own subject knowledge and how it could be improved where appropriate.

Phonological awareness and phonics

It is essential that you have a clear and accurate understanding of what phonics is. It is likely that you will have heard the terms 'analytic' and 'synthetic' phonics used in recent discussions of phonics teaching. You may have considered the programmes you are teaching in relation to these terms.

Some definitions

Phonological awareness can be defined as 'sensitivity to speech at all levels'.

Phonemic awareness can be described as an aspect of phonological awareness. It 'refers more specifically to sounds at the phoneme level' (Graham and Kelly 1997, p. 12).

Synthetic phonics for reading refers to an approach to the teaching of reading in which the phonemes associated with particular graphemes are pronounced in isolation and blended together (synthesised). Synthetic phonics for writing reverses the sequence: pupils are taught to say the word they wish to write, segment it into its phonemes and say them in turn.

Analytic phonics for reading refers to an approach to the teaching of reading in which the phonemes associated with particular graphemes are not pronounced in isolation. Pupils identify (analyse) the common phoneme in a set of words in which each word contains the phoneme under study. Analytic phonics for writing similarly relies on inferential learning (Brooks 2004, CD-ROM).

You can read more about the debate surrounding the effectiveness of various ways of teaching phonics in the Research section of the DfES CD-ROM *Playing with Sounds*. Reading these articles will develop your understanding of the bigger picture of the research, debate and development of the teaching and learning of phonics.

PRACTICAL TASK

- Consider the phonics programme or resource that you use with the whole class.

- Can you identify whether it is based on a synthetic or analytical approach? You may find out more about this by reading the teaching notes or guidance and talking with the literacy or English co-ordinator or the teachers you work with.

- Talk with your literacy/English co-ordinator about the recent debate and the implications for your school.

Developing your own subject knowledge

You will be aware that there is quite a lot of terminology and specific subject knowledge that goes with this area of English. Many of the terms we now use in the teaching of phonics were not used in classrooms when we were children – we learned 'sounds' where teachers now use the correct term 'phoneme' with the pupils. Your own school will have a policy to guide your practice in this. Generally teachers tend to feel that it is important to provide pupils with the correct terms (meta-language) with which to discuss and describe their learning.

PRACTICAL TASK

Use the chart below to audit your understanding of terminology.

TERM	DEFINITION	EXAMPLES
Analogy		
Consonant		
Blend		
Digraph		
Grapheme		
Onset		
Phoneme		
Segment		
Rhyme		
Rime		
Syllable		
Trigraph		
Vowel		

Use the Glossary of terms in the NLS Framework to check.

Follow up any gaps or questions with a teacher or the literacy/English co-ordinator.

In addition to knowing and understanding the terminology used, it is very important that you use exactly the correct sound for each phoneme. Being a correct, clear and consistent model for the pupils you work with is an important aspect of your role as a model for pupils. Your school's literacy or English co-ordinator should be able to recommend another teacher or TA with whom you could check out your use of phonemes. The most common correction that needs to be made is the addition of an 'uh' sound to the end of some phonemes so that 'mmmm' sounds like 'muh' and is then impossible to blend correctly. This is another area where good communication with parents who support with reading at home is essential.

There at least 44 phonemes in the English language. These are represented by combinations of the 26 letters of the alphabet. This means that some letters or combinations of letters represent more than one phoneme (or grapheme when written down). It is essential that you know all of the phonemes. You can check or revise this by consulting the CD-ROM *Playing with Sounds*. In the folder entitled Guidance there is a section called 'Phonics: concepts, knowledge and skills'. Under the knowledge of letters there are two charts:

1. Consonant phonemes and their more usual graphemic representations.
2. Vowel phonemes and their more usual graphemic representations.

Each of these charts shows you the phoneme and some key words that serve as examples. The phonics programme your school uses may have something similar. You may wish to make your own chart using words you think you will remember to use as an *aide-mémoire.*

As a professional TA supporting in literacy and English it would be appropriate for you to be able to identify, pronounce, segment and blend all 44 phonemes.

PRACTICAL TASK

Segment these words into phonemes:

man	tip	crab
m a n		

peg	tent	chimp

jump	cup	snack

You can check the answers for these on the *Playing with Sounds* CD-ROM, in the resources section, Screening: Assessment Task 1.

If you find segmenting challenging, practising with someone regularly for a short time is the key to improving your skills.

What do we teach?

As a professional TA it is important for you to have a good grasp of the developmental stages and age-related expectations. The NLS Framework emphasises the need to teach phonic skills and knowledge at a brisk pace. Early NLS publications such as *Progression in Phonics* (1999) laid out activities to support the teaching and learning of phonological awareness and phonics is a series of steps. More recent publications such as *Playing with Sounds* (2004) have rearranged some of the steps and placed even more emphasis on the need to teach phonics in an interactive, well-paced and engaging way. Schools often have published materials and resources that they use to support in the delivery of a phonics programme.

At the early Foundation Stage (Nursery) the spontaneous and planned play experiences involve experimenting with sounds, being able to articulate and discriminate between sounds heard in English and exploring rhyme and alliteration.

Later in the Foundation Stage (Year R) there is a focus on introducing all letters, learning to segment and blend, reading and writing CVC (consonant-vowel-consonant) words and continued exploring of sounds. Some children may begin to segment and blend consonant digraphs such as *Ch* in 'chat' and *ck* in 'pick'.

In Year 1 daily, interactive work on the letters and phonemes outlined above continues. The reading and writing of vowel digraphs is also introduced in Year 1.

You can explore these stages and expectations more fully using the DfES and commercially published resources that your school uses to ensure that you are familiar with them. This will allow you to plan, teach and assess as well as adapt your teaching and support to the needs of the pupils. In particular, it is important that you know the order in which the class teacher is teaching the phonemes so that you can prompt and support pupils appropriately, knowing which phonemes you can expect them to know and use and which are yet to be taught.

Strategies for teaching phonological awareness and phonics

A recent Ofsted evaluation of effective reading suggested that 'Rapid, early coverage of phonic knowledge and skills ensured that pupils had a strong foundation for decoding' (Ofsted 2005, p. 4) Your role in teaching phonological awareness and phonics may be with the whole class, groups in and out of class including catch-up groups, and/or inividuals with special educational needs. When you are planning, supporting and teaching learning experiences to develop pupils' phonics you should be alert to the use we expect pupils to make of their phonic skills. It should be clear to pupils that they are learning to identify, segment and blend with phonemes in order to use the knowledge and skills in reading and writing. We should also ensure that pupils are learning briskly and interactively.

A balance must be found between the individual and overall sequence of learning objectives with the distractions that may be inherent in activity itself. It is possible for children to be so interested in the games and toys, the rules about using them and waiting for their turn that they lose focus on the learning. Sharing the learning objective and talking with pupils about why they learning phonics is helpful here. Making clear links between phonic skills and their use in reading by explicit modelling in shared, guided and individual reading also makes it clear to pupils why they are learning phonics.

You will recall from reading Chapter 4 that using phonics is one of the searchlight strategies supporting decoding in reading that is described in the NLS Framework. Early phonological work supports pupils in becoming able to hear and distinguish phonemes in English. Some pupils find this quite a challenge. Pupils must then go on to associate each phoneme they hear with the letters that represent it (which in some cases is more than one choice). In order to support their reading they must then be able to segment words into phonemes and blend the phonemes in order to decode a word. At the same time they can use their grammatical, contextual knowledge and their word-recognition skills to support their use of phonic cues. The nature of English means that you must be alert to cues that will most appropriately help the pupil read the word they are working on and help them towards using their phonic skills where they will be most successful. You must also use your knowledge of the pupils' prior attainment, strengths and areas for development to prompt and intervene sensitively.

The recent DfES publication *Playing with Sounds* outlines a coaching and scaffolding approach to use in the teaching of phonics and spelling. These strategies can be very effective when you are supporting pupils with using their phonic skills in reading. At the heart of the coaching and scaffolding approach is the aim to equip pupils with strategies to help themselves when they are stuck. The focus of support is praising pupils for their use of strategies and helping them step by step to independence in decoding. This approach can be modelled in shared and guided reading and can be particularly effective when reading with individuals. Your priority is to identify:

- what the pupil has done right (to be able to praise this)
- how you can best provide the minimum of prompts to support the pupil to correct any errors.

From your experience of reading with pupils you will be aware of many of the typical errors pupils make when they are developing their phonic skills. These include:

SKILL/KNOWLEDGE	EXAMPLE OF ERROR
Segmentation and blending Leaving out a phoneme	The pupil reads 'sand' as 'sad'
Segmentation and blending adding an extra phoneme	The pupil reads 'long' as 'log'
Segmentation and blending segmenting the phonemes in the wrong order	The pupil reads 'curl' as 'crul'
Phonic knowledge not knowing the phoneme for a grapheme	The pupil is reading the word 'bird' Supplies the 'b' and the 'd' but cannot remember 'ir'
Phonic knowledge providing the wrong phoneme for a grapheme	The pupil reads the word 'mail' as 'meal'
Phonic knowledge providing the wrong phoneme for a grapheme in the context of the word	The pupil is reading the word 'flows' in the sentence 'The river flows...' saying the phoneme 'ow' as in 'how'
Visual confusion mixing up two similar phonemes	The pupil reads 'dog' as 'bog'

There are further examples and a series of animations on the DfES CD-ROM *Playing with Sounds*.

Case study

Jonathan is a TA who is supporting Kelly, a Year 2 pupil. Kelly's IEP targets include helping her to use the phonemes she knows when reading and using cues from other searchlights when decoding. Her reliance on contextual clues, and especially picture cues, is causing Kelly to make errors and lose the sense of her reading.

At the start of individual reading sessions Jonathan reminds Kelly that if she gets stuck there are some clues she can use to help her decode the word. He shows her a reminder card based on the searchlights, shown below.

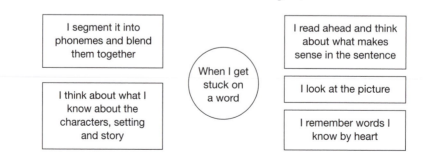

Jonathan refers to this prompt card during reading to help Kelly articulate the cues she is using and show her how she can use two or three cues to help her

> *confirm her decoding of a new word. One of Jonathan's key roles is to prompt
> her to choose searchlight cues that are likely to be effective for the word she is
> aiming to decode. This involves him in scanning ahead, predicting words where
> she may need support and thinking through his prompts.*

In the case study above the TA had developed his understanding of how he
can use the searchlights model to help a pupil who is reading at below the
level expected for her age. He has developed a resource to help her understand
and articulate the cues she can use when reading, with the aim of increasing
the range of cues she uses and gradually improving her independence. Over
time he aims to hand more of this role over to her as she becomes more able
to use a range of cues instead of relying on only one. You might pursue this by
noting some errors you often encounter when reading with pupils and
thinking through why they were made. You could go on to consider the
coaching and scaffolding prompts you could use to support the pupil.

When you provide coaching and scaffolding support the prompts you provide
may not be solely related to phonic skills. You will support pupils in using the
full range of searchlight strategies rather than depending on one strand. In
the examples given above you might prompt pupils to check other
searchlights to see if they confirm their reading or give them the extra cue
they need to self-correct. You should also use your personal knowledge of the
pupil to help you prompt appropriately.

Catch-up programmes

If you support English and literacy in a primary school it is likely that you
have a role in delivering an intervention or catch-up programme with groups
or individuals. There are many programmes available from the DfES, from
LEAs and from publishers. Your own school will have made decisions about
which programme to use to meet the needs of the pupils it serves. Your role in
helping these pupils is crucial, since being a confident and successful reader
and writer is vital to pupils' success in school.

You may have a role in identifying who these pupils are through using
screening checks and other assessments. As you deliver the programme you
will be continually assessing its impact on each pupil in terms of their
learning and their self-esteem. You should also have an awareness of how far
the pupils are using and applying the knowledge, skills and understanding in
their reading and writing in the classroom. You may be in a position to
prompt them to do this and praise them when they do. If you are not able to
do this you should consider who is taking this role in the classroom and
devising an effective and regular way of communicating with them.

It is likely that you are working from a guidance book for the programme you
are delivering. You may also have the opportunity to talk with other TAs and
teachers who are working with the programme in your school and in other
schools. There should be an identified person in your school who is managing
the programme to whom you can go to discuss issues as they occur. You
should be clear about who that person is.

Inevitably, since all children are individuals and their needs rarely overlap completely or seamlessly fit a pre-written programme, there may be times when the programme does not fully meet the needs of the group you are working with. You should be alert to this through your observations and assessments and be ready to adapt aspects of the programme where appropriate. Consulting with the person who is managing the programme would be appropriate.

Working with parents

There are many opportunities to involve parents in supporting their children in using phonics in their reading. Helping parents to understand how schools teach and use phonics in reading can be essential given the changes that have taken place since many parents learned to read. Parents can play an important and positive role in supporting their children's reading and for those children participating in a catch-up programme parental support can be a part of the expectations of the programme. As a school, issues relating to pupils whose parents cannot or will not support them at home will have been thought through to address equal-opportunities issues. Indeed some of your time may be targeted towards pupils receiving less support at home.

Summary

Effective teaching of phonics includes:

- good subject knowledge and an understanding of how pupils develop phonological awareness and phonics in reading
- interactive teaching activities with a clear focus on the learning objective and purpose of the activity
- flexibility in delivery of catch-up programmes to ensure they meet the needs of the identified pupils
- opportunities for pupils to use their phonic skills and knowledge in shared, guided and individual reading with appropriate feedback and support
- clear links between phonological awareness and phonics and the other searchlights.

References

Brooks, G. (2004) *Sounds Sense: The phonics element of the National Literacy Strategy*. Report to the Department for Education and Skills.

Department for Education and Skills (1999) *Progression in Phonics*. London: DfEE

Department for Education and Skills (2004) *Playing With Sounds*. London: DfES

Department for Education and Employment (1999) *Progression in Phonics*. London: DfEE

Graham, J. and Kelly, A. (1998) *Reading Under Control*. London: David Fulton Publishers Ltd

Ofsted (2005) *Reading for Purpose and Pleasure*. An evaluation of the teaching of reading in primary schools. London: Ofsted

7. Spelling

Introduction

The teaching and learning of spelling are closely linked with the development of writing and phonics skills. This chapter should be read in conjunction with the chapters on writing and phonics. You will recall that we discussed writing in relation to composition and transcription. In this chapter we will consider the spelling aspect of transcription. One of the challenges of learning to spell in English is the irregularity of how words are constructed. As Graham and Kelly suggest, the inconsistencies in English can make using spelling rules challenging. It is something that may become more apparent to you as you try to teach pupils to spell. In English we use 26 letters in various combinations to make about 44 phonemes (when said aloud) or graphemes (when written down). But some graphemes represent different sounds in different words, (ow in snow and ow in how) and some graphemes are represented by different combinations of letters, (me, tree, eat, key, happy). Although it is possible to teach spelling rules, there are also exceptions to rules which may be daunting to children.

While you have been considering the teaching and learning of spelling in your own school and any other experiences you have of spelling, perhaps with your own children and in your own education, you may have identified a significant issue for teachers. That is – how do we balance teaching pupils how to spell (the strategies that will equip them to be an independent speller) and teaching pupils to spell specific words and groups of words (key words, irregular words, words that illustrate a pattern, rule or convention). These two threads must be carefully thought through, paying attention to the time spent on them and the impact on pupils' spelling. There may be guidance about this issue in your school policy.

You may be called upon to support pupils who lack confidence in spelling. Being an insecure speller can have a significant impact the pupils' attitude and on the amount and quality of their writing. It is important that we equip pupils with a range of strategies from which to choose when making spelling decisions, including strategies that enable them to continue writing independently rather than get stuck on a word they want to spell and wait until adult support is available. Supporting in such a way that we preserve and enhance self-esteem and a positive attitude is very important here. You will take your lead from the school policy and classroom practice in the school where you work, but it can be useful to have additional strategies available to you to help individuals who are not responding to what the whole class is confident with.

In this chapter we will consider the development of spelling skills up to Year 6. We will explore the strategies that can be used with pupils to help them learn to spell. Developing a positive 'have a go' attitude to spelling will be discussed with consideration about how we help pupils develop independence. This will include a variety of ways of responding to spelling errors and providing appropriate support. In particular, this chapter will focus upon the standards highlighted in the box below.

HLTA STANDARDS

1.1   They have high expectations of all pupils; respect their social, cultural, linguistic, religious and ethnic backgrounds; and are committed to raising their educational achievement.

1.2   They demonstrate and promote the positive values, attitudes and behaviour they expect from pupils with whom they work.

1.5   They are able to liaise sensitively and effectively with parents and carers, recognising their roles in pupils' learning.

2.1   They have sufficient understanding of their specialist area to support pupils' learning, and are able to acquire further knowledge to contribute effectively and with confidence to the classes in which they are involved.

2.2   They are familiar with the school curriculum, the age-related expectations of pupils, the main teaching methods and the testing/examination frameworks in the subjects and age ranges in which they are involved.

2.3   They understand the aims, content, teaching strategies and intended outcomes for the lesson in which they are involved, and understand the place of these in the related teaching programme.

3.1.1 They contribute effectively to teachers' planning and preparation of lessons.

3.1.2 Working within a framework set by the teacher, they plan their role in lessons including how they will provide feedback to pupils and colleagues on pupils' learning and behaviour.

3.3.1 Using clearly structured teaching and learning activities, they interest and motivate pupils, and advance their learning.

3.3.5 They advance pupils' learning in a range of classroom settings, including working with individuals, small groups and whole classes where the assigned teacher is not present.

CHAPTER OBJECTIVES

By the end of this chapter you should:

- have considered your subject knowledge in relation to talking about and teaching spelling
- have familiarised yourself with spelling as it is outlined in the NLS Framework
- have explored a range of strategies for supporting pupils with spelling
- have an understanding of the strategies pupils can use to learn how to spell
- have considered the support necessary for pupils and parents when spelling activities are used for homework.

Developing your own subject knowledge

As with grammar and other areas of English, your own subject knowledge may need to be developed. You may have a good grasp of spelling but need to develop more awareness of how teachers teach spelling and spelling strategies in schools now, or you may feel insecure about your own spelling. It is also important for you to be able to use and understand the language we use to talk about spelling (meta-language), especially if you support pupils in Key Stage 2.

PRACTICAL TASK

Use the chart below to audit your understanding of terminology.

TERM	DEFINITION	EXAMPLES
Affix		
Alliteration		
Compound word		
Discrimination		
Etymology		
Grapheme		
Homonym		
Homophone		
Inflection		
Mnemonic		
Morpheme		
Prefix		
Suffix		
Syllable		

Use the Glossary of terms in the NLS Framework to check.

Follow up any gaps or questions with a teacher or the literacy/English co-ordinator.

What do pupils learn?

It is likely that you are familiar with the objectives for the term and year you most usually work with. Extending this knowledge by looking back and looking ahead will help you develop an understanding of the overall teaching sequence. It will also help you consider where pupils working below or above the level of the majority of the year group are working. This will inform your support by allowing you to prompt and extend pupils effectively.

At Key Stage 1

Phonological awareness, phonics and spelling

Word recognition, graphic knowledge and spelling

At Key Stage 2

Revision and consolidation from Key Stage 1 (to the end of Year 3)

Spelling strategies

Spelling conventions and rules

Use the NLS Framework to identify and track objectives related to spelling.

PRACTICAL TASK

Consider the year and term you are working in now.

Copy and cut out the word-level objectives that relate to spelling and stick them into the chart.

Consult the appropriate appendices to support the objectives.

Identify objectives which are ongoing (e.g. segmenting) and those which are blocked (e.g. specified phonemes, rules, etc.).

Compare them to the teaching sequence, resources and activities in your medium- and short-term planning.

	WORD-LEVEL TERMLY OBJECTIVES FROM THE NLS	RESOURCES AND ACTIVITIES THAT YOU USE
Key Stage 1 Phonological awareness, phonics and spelling **Key Stage 2** Spelling strategies		
Key Stage 1 Word recognition, graphic knowledge and spelling **Key Stage 2** Spelling conventions and rules		

Make connections between what you find and your experience of the pupils you support. You may find it useful to read previous and next objectives in order to support and extend the pupils you are working with.

It is likely that your own school will have made decisions about the order in which specified strategies, phonemes and rules are taught within each term. This may be influenced by the resources your school uses to teach phonics and spelling. It is useful for you to make connections between the termly objectives that underpin planning and the resources and activities that you and the teacher plan and teach.

Supporting pupils with spelling

As a professional TA your role in supporting pupils with their spelling is significant. There will be many occasions when you are working with individuals and groups of pupils who ask you 'How do I spell...?' Your response should be based on a number of factors which may include those related to the school and class approach, the use of resources, the lesson objectives, prior learning in spelling and individual needs in terms of learning and attitude. You may also be supporting pupils in lessons other than English but where writing and spelling are included. You will be using your professional judgement to decide immediately your response to pupils' requests for help. It is useful for you to stand back and consider your instinctive responses thoughtfully and objectively to ensure that the support you give is just right.

School policy and class approach

In supporting pupils with their spelling, as in other areas of English, what you do will be guided by the school policy and how that policy is put into practice in the classrooms you are working in. It is possible that application of the school policy will vary with the age of the pupils and the way individual teachers organise their classrooms. You will be aware of the need for approaching pupils consistently in the classroom. It can be useful to talk with the teachers you are working with to ensure you fully understand their expectations in terms of support for spelling so that you can be consistent in the classrooms where you work.

Resources

It is likely that an aspect of the support available will be related to resources. Schools use a variety of support materials such as word banks, word lists (key words, subject specific words, etc.), visual prompt cards, strategy reminders, word books, dictionaries, etc. Some of these may be planned for use with specific pupils to meet particular needs. It is useful for you to be familiar with the range of support resources, how and when they are used and whether they are for use with specific individuals, groups or the whole class.

Lesson objectives

Your support may be guided by the lesson objectives and may be explicitly stated or implied on the lesson plan. Where the lesson objective is focused on composition, it may be appropriate for you to supply some spellings to allow pupils to write their ideas down using exciting vocabulary rather than being limited to just the words they feel confident about spelling. Your professional judgement and understanding of their prior learning will help you decide which words these are. Where the lesson objective has an emphasis on using spelling rules, conventions or phonemes, your support will be directed towards helping pupils to use what they know to spell the words they are working on.

Pupils' prior learning

As mentioned above, you will be guided by your knowledge of what the pupils have been taught and are secure with using. If you work with particular groups regularly you will probably develop an understanding of where the group's learning is less secure or has gaps, and your expectations for some pupils in the class may be different depending on this accumulated knowledge. For example, if you know that the class are currently working on a group of phonemes (for example, me, tree, eat, key, happy) you will prompt them to practise and use this learning, but if you know they haven't learned 'ough' as in 'enough', you may supply the word 'enough' to them.

Pupils' individual needs

Some of your support may be focused on helping individuals with special educational needs or who are learning English as an additional language. For these pupils you may have received guidance from the class teacher, special educational needs co-ordinator or professionals from outside school regarding support strategies and resources that will be effective. There may be guidance in each pupils' Individual Education Plan or other support programme. This may involve using resources, pre-teaching, working with individuals and groups outside the lesson and liaising with parents.

Pupils' self-esteem

Writing a word down on paper if you are not sure how to spell it is taking a risk for any child, especially a child who is less confident and not happy to take risks. Your support for pupils who are reluctant writers or spellers must include attention to developing a positive attitude, being willing to take risks and boosting self-esteem. A balance must be struck between encouraging independence and keeping up the pace of the writing. Pupils who become dependent on adults for supplying or checking spelling are often paralysed when that level of support is unavailable to them, as inevitably it will be sometimes. The coaching and scaffolding approach described below will help you consider these issues further.

Supporting and teaching in lessons other than English

As a professional TA in a primary school it is likely that you will support or teach pupils in other curriculum areas. You will take into consideration many if not all of the factors outlined above when planning, supporting and teaching in these lessons. It will be important for you to ensure that pupils work at the appropriate level in reading, writing and spelling when recording their work in other subjects. With your knowledge of their learning in English you can prompt them to use their English skills across the curriculum. In terms of spelling, especially in relation to subject-specific vocabulary which may be challenging and beyond the level at which they are spelling, planning and preparation of resources and support materials are essential. This will ensure what the pupils focus is on the new subject learning rather than how to spell subject-specific words.

PRACTICAL TASK

Consider about five lessons that you support or teach in across a week. Try to choose a variety of lessons.

Consider how you will support spelling in each lesson. An example has been included to get you started.

LESSON	LESSON OBJECTIVE	SUPPORT FOR SPELLING
RE	To describe how we feel when we celebrate a special festival.	Usual class prompts, e.g. reminder poster and helping children to use their known strategies and sight words when spelling.

Word lists with picture prompts – names of festivals, range of feelings words.

Is it clear to the pupils you work with what they should do if they can't spell a word?

The coaching and scaffolding approach in spelling

As mentioned earlier in Chapter 6, recent DfES guidance identified a 'coaching and scaffolding approach' to be effective in developing pupils' independence. Effective coaching and scaffolding in spelling involves:

- creating a climate where mistakes are valued and seen as an opportunity for new learning
- identifying exactly what is preventing the pupil from moving on to the next stage
- acknowledging prior learning, promoting self-monitoring and encouraging persistence
- using the minimum amount of support
- leaving the learner feeling satisfaction, boosting their self-esteem and motivation and leaving them with the expectation that they can be successful.

(DfES 2004)

Adopting a coaching and scaffolding style of teaching and feedback in spelling can have a powerful effect on pupils' attitudes to spelling. It requires explicit introduction, consistent implementation and regular modelling by teachers and TAs. You can research this approach further by reading the guidance on the CD-ROM *Playing with Sounds*, where the approach is explained further and demonstrated through a series of short animations.

Case study

Rahana is a TA supporting pupils in Year 2. She has been trained in the coaching and scaffolding approach to spelling and the whole school is implementing it in order to improve pupils' attitudes and willingness to take risks.

Rahana usually works in the same class and has a fairly clear knowledge of the what the class has been taught and the individual needs of the pupils. She has been provided with a class list which gives her an overview of pupils' spelling stages and strategies to use as a quick reminder.

The class teacher Rahana works with indicates to her through her annotated planning when it is appropriate to give pupils feedback on their spelling. In this session Rahana is working her way round a group of eight pupils identifying some errors and giving coaching and scaffolding feedback to them.

When Rahana looks at the pupils' writing she firstly identifies spelling errors with the pupils. She does not identify every spelling mistake. She uses her knowledge of the pupils' learning to identify those words it is reasonable to expect them to be able to spell using their current knowledge, skills and understanding. She also asks the pupils themselves to choose words they would like feedback on.

In order to coach and scaffold Rahana firstly acknowledges where the word is spelled correctly by highlighting. For example, where Jasmin has spelled 'brown' as 'broun' she highlights br and n and praises Jasmin for choosing the right letters for the start and end of the word. She also praises her for choosing a phoneme that represents 'ou' although in this instance it is the wrong choice. Rahana draws Jasmin's attention to the other phoneme choices and asks her try them out and then check in the dictionary to find the correct one.

In the case study outlined above Rahana coaches and scaffolds the pupils little and often. She does not identify and address every single spelling error but uses her professional judgement of the pupils to choose those instances that are most appropriate to the pupils' current progress. She has found that as she gives this explicit and clear positive feedback and scaffolding, the pupils begin to internalise the support and use it in their independent spelling. Pupils are becoming clear about the sorts of strategies that are successful when trying to spell a new word and this is improving their confidence and willingness to have a go.

Strategies for spelling

There are a number of strategies that we can teach pupils to support spelling. These include the following.

Segmenting words into phonemes

As pupils in Years R, 1 and 2 learn phonemes and how to blend and segment words into phonemes, this strategy can be very helpful. Teaching pupils how to listen to, identify and be able write each phoneme systematically can support the spelling of mainly regular words. For example, a pupil in the middle of Year 1 might segment the word 'scratch' as 's...c...r...a...t...ch'.

Choosing the appropriate phoneme/grapheme

As pupils try to spell more challenging words by segmenting, they have to make the correct choice of phoneme for the word they want to spell. For example, a pupil in the middle of Year 2 might segment the word 'cloud' into its phonemes 'c...l...ou...d' and then have to make the choice between the graphemes 'ou' and 'ow'. In order to make choices, pupils need to develop a grasp of the groups of graphemes that might represent a phoneme, perhaps by recalling a key word and picture for each one.

Visual recall

As pupils' experience of the English language increases, they will develop a 'feel' for what looks right. Some pupils will always find this very challenging, but where pupils can use this instinct it is a useful strategy. Presenting and sorting words into groups, sets and lists can help to develop this feel. Some pupils also find designing their own calligrams for tricky words can give them the additional mental image that they need.

Rhyme and analogy

Using rhyme and analogy to make connections between groups of words helps pupils begin to generalise and apply this learning to other words. For example, if pupils can spell 'light' they can also spell 'right, flight, sight...' although in English there are always exceptions, analogy can still be a useful strategy.

Mnemonics

Some pupils find that devising or using an existing mnemonic for longer words that they have trouble remembering can be helpful. An example of this could be for 'because': **b**ig **e**lephants **c**an **a**lways **u**nderstand **s**mall **e**lephants.

Spelling rules and conventions

As stated by Graham and Kelly, 'rules are only useful when they apply to a large number of words, when there are few exceptions and when they are easily understood' (1998, p. 80).

The word-level objectives in the NLS Framework outline the spelling rules and conventions that pupils are taught.

The structure of words (morphology)

Teaching pupils about the roots of words, the part of the word that does not change, can help them see patterns in spelling. Learning the effect of adding prefixes and suffixes, making words into plurals and changing tenses all support spelling.

Word meanings (etymology)

As pupils get older and their vocabulary and awareness of the English language develops, we can help them make connections based on the origin and history of words. Pupils are often interested in these groups of words and also words that English has absorbed from other countries.

Clearly there is a variety of strategies pupils can use to help them spell the words they need for their writing. As pupils move through Key Stage 2 they will have been introduced to this range. The challenge is then to guide pupils towards choosing an appropriate strategy to fit the word the pupil wants to spell, since some strategies are more appropriate for some types of words. For example, choosing a segmenting strategy to spell a very phonically irregular word would be an inappropriate choice. In addition, as pupils get older it will become apparent that some strategies suit their learning styles more than others. For example, a pupil with a good visual memory may rely on recall of visual patterns whereas a pupil who learns in a more auditory style may be more successful with using sounds, rhymes, word play and mnemonics.

As a professional TA you have a role in helping pupils choose the appropriate strategies for the words they need to spell. You may be involved in helping pupils develop and use a spelling log or journal at Key Stage 2. Using a spelling log effectively can be a useful support for pupils in learning, choosing and applying strategies. A spelling log may contain:

- words that the pupil has spelled incorrectly, along with the corrected spelling and a strategy for learning to spell the word
- examples of strategies to work spelling or learn specific words
- spelling investigations and the generalisations that result from them

- spelling conventions and rules and examples of them
- word meanings, words with linked meanings, dictionary work
- lists of subject-specific key words
- spelling activities
- individual and class targets related to spelling
- homework activities.

Spelling logs will be a combination of personal and class work and should be used as a tool within the class in English and in other lessons.

Spelling as homework

In many schools pupils throughout Key Stages 1 and 2 take spelling activities home as part of their homework. This may be to practise class, group or individual spellings or lists of words, collect examples of words containing the phonemes, rules or conventions that the pupils are using or games and investigations using words pupils are currently learning or consolidating. Older pupils may use their spelling journal at home for this practice. As with any homework it is important that parents understand the purpose of the work and how they can best support their pupils with it. You may be called upon to ensure that parents, especially of younger pupils, can support their pupils at home. You may talk with them at the beginning or end of the day, use a homework diary, contribute to training sessions or meetings or prepare information to send home. A priority when setting spelling activities as homework is that they are purposeful and clearly linked to classroom learning.

Summary

Effective teaching of spelling includes:

- good subject knowledge and an understanding of how pupils develop spelling knowledge and strategies
- interactive teaching activities with a clear focus on the learning objective and purpose of the activity
- opportunities for pupils to use their phonic skills and knowledge in shared and guided writing with appropriate feedback and support
- communication with parents where spelling is set as a homework activity.

References

Department for Education and Employment (1998) *The National Literacy Strategy Framework for teaching.* London: DfEE

Department for Education and Skills (2001) *Year 7 Spelling Bank.* London: DfES

Department for Education and Skills (2004) *Playing With Sounds.* London: DfES

Graham, J. and Kelly, A. (1998a) *Reading Under Control.* London: David Fulton

Graham, J. and Kelly, A. (1998b) *Writing Under Control.* London: David Fulton

8. Grammar and punctuation

Introduction

You will have noticed that there is ongoing debate about why, what and how grammar should be taught in schools and what the impact of teaching or not teaching it is on pupils' learning of English. Your own attitude towards the teaching of grammar may have been formed by your experiences as a learner. You may have been taught grammar very formally without connection to its use in your speaking and listening, reading and writing. You may have experienced no formal and identifiable teaching of grammar in your own experience as a pupil. If you are a native English speaker, your understanding and use of grammar may be instinctive and based on your experience and use of the English language. If you have learned to speak other languages, your experience of learning grammar in these languages may have caused you to think about and make connections with grammar in English.

Your most recent learning about grammar and punctuation may have been to review and revise your own knowledge and understanding in order to support the pupils you are teaching accurately and effectively. As a professional TA it is essential that you do develop your own subject knowledge in this area at and beyond the level at which the pupils you support are working at. It is likely that you will work with pupils who need to be extended – you must be a position to do this effectively. You must also consider your own role as a model for the pupils you work with. The way you use words, construct and punctuate sentences and make meaning in English will have an impact.

In this chapter we will consider what grammar is, how punctuation is used and the aspects and elements of grammar and punctuation that we are required to teach at Key Stages 1 and 2. You will be encouraged to audit and extend your own subject knowledge in relation to grammar and punctuation to ensure that you can support at levels appropriate to the pupils you work with. We will explore the strategies teachers use to teach grammar and punctuation including those which are implicit and those which are explicit. Using knowledge about grammar in speaking and listening, reading and writing will be part of this. In particular, this chapter will focus upon the standards highlighted in the box below.

HLTA STANDARDS

1.1 They have high expectations of all pupils; respect their social, cultural, linguistic, religious and ethnic backgrounds; and are committed to raising their educational achievement.

1.2 They demonstrate and promote the positive values, attitudes and behaviour they expect from pupils with whom they work.

2.1 They have sufficient understanding of their specialist area to support pupil's learning, and are able to acquire further knowledge to contribute effectively and with confidence to the classes in which they are involved.

2.2 They are familiar with the school curriculum, the age-related expectations of pupils, the main teaching methods and the testing/examination frameworks in the subjects and age ranges in which they are involved.

2.3 They understand the aims, content, teaching strategies and intended outcomes for the lesson in which they are involved, and understand the place of these in the related teaching programme.

3.1.1 They contribute effectively to teachers' planning and preparation of lessons.

3.1.2 Working within a framework set by the teacher, they plan their role in lessons including how they will provide feedback to pupils and colleagues on pupil's learning and behaviour.

3.3.1 Using clearly structured teaching and learning activities, they interest and motivate pupils, and advance their learning.

3.3.5 They advance pupil's learning in a range of classroom settings, including working with individuals, small groups and whole classes where the assigned teacher is not present.

CHAPTER OBJECTIVES

By the end of this chapter you should:

● know more about what grammar is and some of the current research about grammar teaching and learning

● be aware of the requirements for the teaching of grammar and punctuation at Key Stages 1 and 2

● have developed an understanding of the range of strategies for the teaching of grammar and punctuation skills that teachers use

● have considered your own subject knowledge and how it could be improved where appropriate.

What is grammar?

Your perception of what 'grammar' is will be related to your experience as a pupil, student and TA. You may have memories of explicit grammar exercises that seemed to have no relation to your reading and writing or you may have been taught grammar implicitly within other learning so that you feel you have had no formal instruction at all in this area. The word 'grammar' can also carry with it ideas about social class and the way people speak and write, which may affect the way you feel about it.

In terms of teaching and learning of English in schools today it is important to be guided by the aim of improving our pupils' speaking and listening, reading and writing. Ensuring that pupils know and can use the correct terminology (or meta-language) when talking about the English language gives them the tools with which they can develop their thinking about language. Encouraging pupils to evaluate the effects of the words, sentences and paragraphs they read and write enables them to make a wider range of choices. Ensuring that pupils explore the grammar appropriate to different forms of writing enables them to write more effectively in that genre.

In *Grammar for Writing* it is suggested that at Key Stages 1 and 2 grammar is concerned with:

- text cohesion
- sentence construction and punctuation
- word choice and modification.

(DfEE 2000, p.10)

When we look at references to grammar in the programme of study in the English National Curriculum we find it in the following places:

- En1 Speaking and Listening – 5 Standard English and 6 Language variation
- En2 Reading – 1 Reading strategies and 4 Language structure and variation
- En3 Writing – 6 Standard English and 7 Language structure

In addition to these sources of information very much more specific objectives are outlined in the NLS Framework at word, sentence and text levels.

Although we most clearly see the effects of the teaching of grammar in writing, it also has a place in the teaching of speaking and listening and in reading. When we talk we can more readily use the context, facial expression, gesture and intonation to convey meaning and create effect. When we write we must use more explicit grammatical structures and organisational features to communicate our ideas (DfEE 2000, p.8). When we read we use our grammatical understanding to help us predict, self-correct and read with expression. It is important to pass on knowledge of grammar in such a way that it helps to make the pupils 'more discriminating readers, writers and speakers and empowers them to produce written and spoken texts which both embody what it is they want to say and make a suitable impact on those listening or reading' (Wilson 2001, p.52).

What is punctuation?

When we are speaking we are able to use intonation, pauses, gesture and facial expression to ensure that our meaning is clear to the listener. When we are writing we use punctuation to indicate some of this meaning to the reader. For example, when we are reading a piece of written text aloud, the placing of a comma tells us to pause, and the use of exclamation marks and question marks help us judge the tone in which to read. Punctuation also allows us to make clear the boundaries of phrases, clauses, sentences and speech.

Developing your subject knowledge

The aspects and elements of grammar and punctuation that we teach are outlined in the National Curriculum Handbook. Further more detailed objectives for each term are provided in the NLS Framework. As a professional TA you can use these to consider your own subject knowledge and check that you understand and can use the aspects of grammar and punctuation you are teaching and supporting in. This can form a basis from which can you can further ensure that your knowledge and understanding of grammar and punctuation are developed beyond that of the pupils you teach. You may find that as you do this it is the terminology to describe the language we use that you are learning, rather than new grammatical features.

PRACTICAL TASK

Use the programme of study for Key Stage 2 to begin your self-audit. Check that you know, can define and give examples of each of the grammatical features listed. Try to identify examples of each feature in a familiar text.

NATIONAL CURRICULUM KS 2	YOUR OWN SUBJECT KNOWLEDGE
En3 (7) Language Structure Pupils should be taught:	
a. Word classes and grammatical functions of words, including nouns, verbs, adjectives, pronouns, prepositions, conjunctions, articles.	
b. The features of different types of sentences, including statements, questions and commands, and how to use them.	
c. The grammar of complex sentences, including clauses, phrases and connectives.	
d. The purposes and organisational features of paragraphs, and how ideas can be linked.	

▶

Resources for improving subject knowledge in grammar are readily available online and in the form of textbooks for pupils, students and teachers. Some that you might consider are:

- www.standards.dfes.gov.uk/primary/profdev/literacy/571599/

Five self-study modules provided by the DfES. They review key grammatical concepts for use by TA and teachers who want to update their grammatical knowledge.

- www.standards.dfes.gov.uk/primary/publications/literacy/63321/

Three leaflets summarising the grammatical content of the National Literacy Strategy course *Grammar for Writing.*

1. From word to sentence
2. From sentence to text
3. From grammar to writing

Searching the internet will provide you with references to many websites that address grammar for pupils, students and teachers.

- Pupil textbooks such as:

Gee, R. and Watson, C. (1983) *The Usborne Guide to English Grammar.* London: Usborne

Gee, R. and Watson, C. (1983) *The Usborne Guide to English Punctuation.* London: Usborne

You might find textbooks written with pupils in mind an accessible way in to developing your subject knowledge.

- Student teacher/teacher textbooks such as:

Wilson, A. (2001) *Language Knowledge for Primary Teachers.* London: David Fulton

Eyres, I. (2000) *Primary English. Developing Subject Knowledge.* London: Open University

In addition to grammar you should also be clear about the introduction and use of punctuation from Years 1 to 6. In order to develop an understanding of the sequence and contexts in which punctuation is taught in the NLS

Framework, you can systematically look through the sentence-level objectives at the section entitled 'Sentence construction and punctuation'.

Grammar and punctuation

PRACTICAL TASK

Use the NLS Framework sentence-level objectives.

Identify when aspects of punctuation are introduced and any contextual information to support this as in the example below.

YEAR	SENTENCE-LEVEL OBJECTIVE	SUPPORTING INFORMATION
3	Term 1 S6 To secure the use of questions marks and exclamation marks Term 1 S7 To learn the basic conventions of speech punctuation Term 1 S8 To use the term 'speech marks'	in reading, understand their purpose and use appropriately in own reading through identifying speech marks in reading beginning to use in own writing using capital letters to mark the start of direct speech

You may find it useful to choose one aspect of punctuation, such as commas, and trace references to this from Years 1 to 6. This will give you an opportunity to identify what pupils have been taught before and see the next steps in teaching.

While revising and developing your understanding of punctuation you might use Module 5 of the self-study units available at

www.standards.dfes.gov.uk/primary/profdev/literacy/571599/

You can also consolidate your understanding by finding examples of each type of punctuation in familiar texts. This will allow you to feel confident about helping pupils identify, describe and use punctuation in reading and writing.

Strategies for teaching grammar and punctuation

When we think about teaching grammar we can teach it as it naturally occurs within speaking and listening, reading and writing activities (implicitly) and we can also teach specific parts of it separately (explicitly). The challenge for teachers and TAs is to plan a balanced programme of learning activities that have at the heart of them the aim of improving pupils' English. We cannot rely on all of the grammatical features we need to teach appearing in the course of teaching. We must choose texts and other language learning experiences that support the pupils' learning of grammar. Although discrete grammar activities have a place in teaching and learning they must be clearly and coherently linked to speaking and listening, reading and writing contexts. You may be able to address this link through your use of clear learning intentions and success criteria.

93

PRACTICAL TASK

Over two weeks observe the instances when aspects of grammar are taught. This may be in whole-class, group or individual contexts and it may be in speaking and listening, reading or writing.

Consider whether the teaching is implicit (in relation to a text or the pupils' own speaking, reading or writing) or explicit (a specific feature taught and practised on its own).

ASPECT OF GRAMMAR	IMPLICIT TEACHING	EXPLICIT TEACHING
Week 1		
Week 2		

Talk with teachers about the rationale behind the planning of the teaching of grammar in the classrooms you work in.

Is it clear to you and the pupils how their grammatical learning is linked to their reading, writing, speaking and listening?

Clearly as pupils move through Key Stage 2 the grammatical knowledge demanded of them will develop and become more complex as pupils become more competent, confident and experienced in their use of English. Unless you are very confident of your grasp of the grammatical features that you are working with it is useful for you anticipate what the pupils will be learning by looking ahead at planning. This will give the opportunity to check your subject knowledge, consider what the pupils already need know and investigate resources.

Case study

Kerry is a TA supporting in a Year 3 class. Kerry works with a group who need additional support with reading and writing and working just below the level expected for their age and year group. In term 2 some of the sentence level work is based around objective S2.

Pupils should be taught:

The function of adjectives within sentences, through:

- *identifying adjectives in shared reading*

- *discussing and defining what they have in common*

- *experimenting with deleting and substituting adjectives and noting effects on meaning*

- *collecting and classifying adjectives*

- *experimenting with the impact of different adjectives through shared writing.*

As this work approaches Kerry considers her own subject knowledge in relation to the objective. She feels secure with this area of grammar (word classes).

She goes on consider the objectives in relation to what she knows about the pupils she supports, in particular whether the pupils have solid prior knowledge about nouns and which adjectives will be appropriate to the reading levels of the pupils she is supporting.

She investigates the texts the teacher has planned to use so she can identify where they support these objectives. She collects sets of adjectives related to size, colour and appearance so that when she works with the pupils she can be ready to prompt and guide them.

During the teaching that relates to this objective Kerry's thorough preparation allows her to support shared reading effectively. Kerry helps some pupils access these sessions by pre-teaching so that these pupils have the opportunity to become familiar with the focus passages before working with the whole class to identify adjectives. She is also able to follow up in guided and individual reading sessions where appropriate.

As she prepared for the series of lessons Kerry felt that it would be essential that the group she works with understand the way adjectives are used – to describe, to tell us more about nouns. She devises some speaking and listening activities where pupils are challenged to describe objects/book characters using as many adjectives as possible or to describe one object/book character using precisely chosen adjectives in order to distinguish it from a group. These are popular with all the pupils, although they were planned for one group.

In this case study it is clear that the consideration Kerry gave to her own subject knowledge and the pupils' prior knowledge helped her to support and teach effectively. Her research into texts, groups of adjectives and speaking and listening activities has ensured that the pupils she supports have additional support and prompts. She finds that this work is of value to the whole class. She discusses with the teacher the planning of teaching activities that are implicit, using text in shared reading and writing; alongside more explicit and discrete activities where the pupils collect, classify and use adjectives. She is also aware that it will be important to ensure that the pupils make effective choices from the adjectives they know in order to improve their writing as well as understanding the types of writing where the use of adjectives is appropriate and will enhance the writing.

Recent research suggests that some of the most effective experiences for the teaching of grammar are those referred to as 'sentence combining' (The English Review Group 2004, p.6). Sentence combining can be defined as manipulating phrases and clauses to write more complex sentences. Sentence combining can include such activities as:

- Sentence expansion – adding additional words, phrases and clauses.
- Sentence reduction – taking away words to reduce the sentence to its simplest form.
- Sentence transformation – changing one word at a time, changing tenses, singular to plural, etc.
- Sentence matching – matching words to an existing sentence.
- Sentence completion/stems – supplying a missing beginning or end, often using conjunctions.
- Sentence modelling – making up similar sentences to a model.
- Sentence comparison – comparing versions of sentences.

(adapted from Dewsbury 1997)

Some of these types of activities are also suggested and outlined in *Grammar for Writing* such as expansion (p.44) and re-ordering (p.90). When set within meaningful contexts the practical nature of sentence-combining activities and the discussion and decision-making involved can be effective in helping pupils to learn and improve their English. It can also be planned to give pupils the opportunity to consider their own writing as a context.

Case study

Carl works with pupils in later Key Stage 2, providing support for writing in particular. Some pupils have been identified who have a need in common. They tend to write in long and complicated sentences that do not always make sense. Carl has been asked to work with this group for a series of short lessons with a focus on strategies for writing simple, compound and complex sentences that make sense.

> *Carl has recently read about ways of reducing, expanding and manipulating sentences which he thinks will help the pupils begin to take control of their own unwieldy sentences. He bases his teaching activities on a combination of the pupils' own writing (where they volunteer), his own writing and texts currently being used in the classes the pupils work in. He uses resources that encourage participation such as sticky notes, cards, write-on-wipe-off boards and enlarged photocopies. Discussion, explanation, evaluation, re-reading and checking for sense are important aspects of his lessons. He is aiming for the pupils to be able to evaluate their work independently as they write, back in the classroom, rather than writing indiscriminately aiming for length rather than quality.*

The case study presented above demonstrates the significance of making links between what pupils read, their own writing and learning about grammar. Carl is able to support pupils to revise specific features of knowledge about grammar and use these features more effectively and appropriately in their own writing until they become part of their writing repertoire.

When we teach pupils to use punctuation, similar strategies can be used. We can identify examples of the punctuation mark in shared reading, begin to generalise about how it is used on the basis of our experiences in reading and use it in our own writing. In shared and guided writing you and the teacher will be explicitly modelling decisions about what punctuation to include and the effect of making changes; for example, using an exclamation mark instead of a full stop. It can be useful to provide pupils with a visual reminder of the punctuation they should be consistently including through using posters such as the example below or a very effective visual image – the punctuation pyramid (Wilson 2001, p.35).

As pupils accumulate knowledge about punctuation they can be reminded of it by using posters.These can be made more meaningful when illustrated with examples from familiar texts and their own writing. They can be used as revision aids and prompts to activate prior knowledge before building on that previous learning. They can be passed on to the next class with the pupils to use as a transition aid.

The punctuation pyramid is a very useful visual reminder to pupils of the punctuation that they have learned to use so far. It can also be used in target setting and helping pupils move on and improve their writing. Each layer represents the punctuation expectations at one National Curriculum level with Level 1 at the top.

!!!!!!!!!!!!!!!!!!!!!!

We use exclamation marks

In reading

To read aloud using the expression the writer wants us to use

In writing

To tell the reader that it is a shock or a surprise

!!!!!!!!!!!!!!!!!!!!!!!!

The Punctuation Pyramid

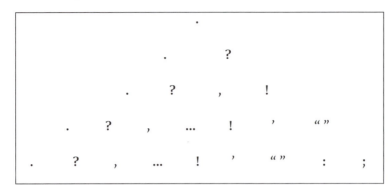

(Wilson 2001, p35)

Summary

Effective teaching of grammar and punctuation includes:

- good subject knowledge about grammar and punctuation
- interactive teaching activities with a clear focus on the learning objective and purpose of the activity
- opportunities for pupils to use their grammatical skills and knowledge in shared and guided writing with appropriate feedback and support
- clear links between explicit and implicit learning.

References

Department for Education and Employment (1998) *The National Literacy Strategy Framework for Teaching*. London: DfEE

Department for Education and Employment (1999) *The National Curriculum Handbook for Primary Teachers in England*. London: DfEE

Department for Education and Employment (2000) *Grammar for Writing*. London: DfEE

Dewsbury, A. (1997) *First Steps. Writing Resource Book*. Victoria: Rigby Heinemann

The English Review Group (2004) *The Effect of Grammar Teaching (Sentence Combining) in English on 5 to 16 Year Olds' Accuracy and Quality in Written Composition*. London: EPPI

Wilson, A. (2001) *Language Knowledge for Primary Teachers*. London: David Fulton

Wilson, R. (2001) *Raising Standards in Writing*. Huddersfield: Kirklees School Effectiveness Service

9. Handwriting

Introduction

When we teach handwriting to pupils we are aiming to help them develop a legible and fluent handwriting style that allows them to write at speed. While this is likely to be based on a school-adopted style, as pupils get older there may be some scope for developing individualities within it. As a professional TA your own handwriting should display the features that you are teaching to pupils and be a good model of your school's handwriting style. This may require some practice.

In this chapter we will consider the issues you need to take into consideration in relation to your own handwriting in order to be able to support and teach handwriting. We will investigate what pupils are taught in Key Stages 1 and 2 and consider some teaching strategies. In particular, this chapter will focus upon the standards highlighted in the box below.

HLTA STANDARDS

1.1   They have high expectations of all pupils; respect their social, cultural, linguistic, religious and ethnic backgrounds; and are committed to raising their educational achievement.

1.2   They demonstrate and promote the positive values, attitudes and behaviour they expect from pupils with whom they work.

2.1   They have sufficient understanding of their specialist area to support pupil's learning, and are able to acquire further knowledge to contribute effectively and with confidence to the classes in which they are involved.

2.2   They are familiar with the school curriculum, the age-related expectations of pupils, the main teaching methods and the testing/examination frameworks in the subjects and age ranges in which they are involved.

2.3   They understand the aims, content, teaching strategies and intended outcomes for the lesson in which they are involved, and understand the place of these in the related teaching programme.

3.1.1   They contribute effectively to teachers' planning and preparation of lessons.

3.3.1   Using clearly structured teaching and learning activities, they interest and motivate pupils, and advance their learning.

CHAPTER OBJECTIVES

By the end of this chapter you should:

- be aware of the expectations for handwriting at Key Stages 1 and 2
- have considered the range of skills that contribute to developing a legible and fluent handwriting style that can be used at speed
- have considered areas for your own development in relation to providing effective support for handwriting.

Developing your own subject knowledge and skills

Whatever subjects or lessons you are supporting in, it will be important that you have an understanding of how pupils are taught handwriting skills. In addition to finding out more about what the National Curriculum requires and the NLS Framework recommends, it is essential to clarify the expectations of your school. Information about your school's approach to handwriting will probably be part of the English policy or a policy document in its own right. It is likely that you will be able get a feel for what this policy is by looking at the labels on displays around the school, the teachers' writing on whiteboards, looking the pupils' writing at different stages and the supporting resources available for handwriting.

PRACTICAL TASK

Use your school handwriting policy, observations of teaching and evidence around the school to ensure that you know the school's aims in each of the areas.

Identify any areas for personal development.

	YOUR SCHOOL POLICY	NOTES
Individual letter formation		
When pupils begin to join		
How letters are joined		
Developing a personal style		
Posture, grip		
Use of supporting resources such as guide lines, use of pens, etc.		
Left-handed pupils		
Pupils joining the school		
Pupils with SEN		
Teaching organisation and strategies		
Use of published materials		

You may need to watch another adult forming and joining letters to fully understand how the handwriting style is used.

Although handwriting is a skill requiring physical co-ordination and control of a pencil or pen, it is important that you understand the experiences and activities that can contribute to the development of gross and fine motor control generally. This will give you the scope to plan handwriting activities that are creative and motivating for pupils, especially those pupils who find pencil control challenging.

Gross motor control is related to developing control of our body, arms and legs. In terms of handwriting, pupils need to develop good arm control, body posture and balance. Fine motor control is related to developing control of smaller movements. For handwriting pupils need to develop control of their hand and fingers. Pupils also need to develop strength in their hands and fingers to be able to grip and manipulate a pen or pencil. When you are planning activities to develop handwriting including activities to develop this range of areas can have a positive impact on handwriting. Section 3 in the DfES publication *Developing Early Writing* (2001) will give you further guidance and ideas about developing handwriting, especially with younger pupils.

What do pupils learn?

At the Foundation Stage experiences that support the development of handwriting are outlined in the Communication, Language and Literacy area of learning.

The stepping stones are as follows:

- Engage in activities requiring hand–eye co-ordination
- Use one-handed tools and equipment
- Draw lines and circles using gross motor movement
- Manipulate objects with increasing control
- Begin to use anticlockwise movement and retrace vertical lines
- Begin to form recognisable letters
- Use a pencil and hold it effectively to form recognisable letters, most of which are correctly formed.

(QCA 2000)

It is useful, especially if you are teaching and supporting at Key Stage 1, to know about these early activities. There will be many pupils who still need gross and fine motor control development in order to support their progress in handwriting. What pupils are taught in handwriting is specified in the National Curriculum. You can read En3 to check that you know what the statutory requirements are. The NLS Framework supplies termly objectives until the end of Year 4, when pupils should have developed a legible, fluent style in which they can write at speed.

At Key Stage 1

Year 1

- Develop a comfortable pencil grip.
- Form lowercase letters correctly in a script that will be easy to join later.
- Use correct letter orientation, formation and proportion (linked to spelling and independent writing).

Year 2

- Introduce and practise the four basic handwriting joins.

At Key Stage 2

Year 3

- Consolidate the four basic handwriting joins.
- Ensure consistency in size, proportions of letters and spacing between letters.
- Build up handwriting speed, fluency, legibility through practice.

Year 4

- Use joined handwriting all the time except when specific forms require printing.
- Know when to use a clear, neat hand for finished work or more informal writing for drafting, notes, etc.
- Use a range of presentational skills (summarised from the NLS Framework 2001).

Strategies for teaching handwriting

The practical task above will have helped you find out more about the school expectations and resources for the teaching of handwriting. As a professional TA you may be supporting or teaching handwriting with the whole class, with groups or with individuals, especially those experiencing difficulties with handwriting. Your decisions about how to teach and support will be influenced by the way your teaching is organised.

With a whole class or group

If you have observed handwriting being taught, you will know that where letter formation or joins are demonstrated to large groups of pupils, holding the attention of all pupils can be difficult. For some pupils in a larger group it is not realistic to expect them to hold the letter formation in their head after being shown at a distance and then reproduce this correctly when they practise. When planning to demonstrate and model aspects of handwriting to a large group of pupils it is important to think through how they will interact and join in, in order to learn effectively. This can be addressed through the pupils each having a little whiteboard and pen and working along with the teacher or TA, articulating what you are doing with the pupils joining in, and asking them to copy movements on a large scale in the air.

Case study

Judy is a TA who works with a Year 1 and 2 class. She helps to plan for and resources the regular handwriting sessions for the class. The class teacher and Judy plan the objectives for each session. These will be taught to small groups, allowing for differentiation.

In addition to this focused work Judy plans supplementary activities to develop fine motor skills. She has developed a bank of these including using pegs and boards, sewing cards, threading beads, cutting along lines and shapes, controlling the cursor on the screen using a mouse, using play dough, and pattern making. As well as finding these activities fun the pupils are challenged to improve their control of tools, their finger strength and their grip.

In addition to this Judy plans one large-scale scribbling activity to support the focused objective. This might be making lines or zig-zags from left to right to support the development of joined script, scribbling round and round to emphasise the direction of letters such as c, a, o, and d, or making up and down marks to improve 'tall' letters such as l, h, b, and k. Working on a large scale, emphasising large arm movements and directions seems to help some of the pupils, especially those who have a tendency to write in a small, hesitant and constricted way.

Within this session the class teacher and Judy have the opportunity to teach focused groups and ensure that each pupil receives some direct teaching and feedback at the appropriate level as well practising their fine and gross motor skills.

In the case study above the class teacher and TA consider it appropriate and practical to teach handwriting though a rotation of small groups, planning activities to promote gross and fine motor development for the rest of the class as well as focused teaching for groups. Judy's involvement in the planning of these sessions allows her to go on to plan supporting activities which will fit with the specific skills being taught. Her knowledge of the needs of individuals allows her to build in some targeted support for pupils who need the opportunity to develop particular skills.

With individuals

If you are supporting individuals with handwriting it is likely that they are experiencing some challenge in this area. You may have been given guidance through the pupils' Individual Education Plan or from outside professionals who will support your work. If the school timetable and organisation allows you, short, regular inputs are likely to be more effective than longer periods of time less often. Ensuring that the pupil uses the skills you are teaching and practising in their usual work is also important. You may get the opportunity to remind, prompt and praise if you also work in the classroom as well as support individually. If the pupil is using specific support resources to help with their handwriting (such as a pencil grip, triangular pen, guidelines, posture guide), it is important that you and the teacher consider how the pupil feels and how these resources are presented within the class. It may be more tactful to have these resources available for all rather than centred upon one pupil who may then resist being different or feel exposed.

Joined handwriting

Schools vary in their decisions about when to introduce joined handwriting. The NLS Framework recommends that the print script that the pupils use should be one that will be easy to join later and introduces joins in Year 2. It is essential that you follow the school policy and any scheme that your school uses so that you are consistent. Exploring how each letter is joined and practising key words may be useful if the handwriting style is new to you.

Left-handed pupils

Developing a fluent and legible handwriting style can be a particular challenge for left-handed pupils. When you are supporting left-handed pupils you might consider issues such as:

- Position – the pupil will need space to move at his or her left. You may need to consider where pupils are sitting in relation to each other so they do not jog each other.
- Paper – the paper or handwriting book needs to be positioned to the left of the body and slanted to the right.
- Pencils and pens – it is essential that the writing implement flows since a left-handed pupil is often pushing the pencil or pen. When writing with a pen you might consider pens designed for left-handers which help them overcome smudging and grip.

The website **www.anythinglefthanded.co.uk** has a range of products which may be helpful, including pens, scissors and video.

Using handwriting skills

As with any skill that we teach it is crucial that we also ensure that pupils use and apply the skill in their usual work. It is very easy for pupils to produce handwriting of a good standard in their handwriting books when they are fully focused on handwriting but for there to be less evidence of this in their other exercise books. On the other hand, you will have found that if you focus on handwriting in other lessons the focus will be shifted from the learning in that subject to the presentation and handwriting.

Giving handwriting and presentation a high profile around the school can help make it clear to pupils the standards and expectations. Arranging competitions and displays, joining in with national events and promoting good models of handwriting can also be effective.

Working with parents

Many schools share their handwriting style with parents to encourage them to help pupils with writing in a way that will fit with the school approach. This is another aspect of English where clear communication with parents can be beneficial for school and the child. You may have opportunities to develop this communication when talking with parents about reading, phonics and spelling. Explaining clearly what the school expectations are about when joined handwriting is introduced, when pupils begin using pens, the sorts of guidelines pupils use and other issues can pre-empt confusion and concern.

A useful resource is 'My write-well mat' available from **www.formative-fun.com**. This provides some child-friendly reminders about grip, letter formation, posture and position of the paper with a left-hander version on one side and a right-hander version on the other. This can be useful both at home and at school.

Summary

Effective teaching of handwriting is dependent upon:

- providing pupils with a clear, consistent model
- planning a programme that develops gross and fine motor control as well as specific handwriting skills
- ensuring pupils use and apply the skills they use in all writing
- providing appropriate specific support for pupils who find handwriting challenging.

References

Department for Education and Employment (1998) *The National Literacy Strategy Framework for Teaching*. London: DfEE

Department for Education and Employment (1999) *The National Curriculum Handbooks for Primary Teachers in England*. London: DfEE

Department for Educations and Skills (2001) *Developing Early Writing*. London: DfES

QCA (2000) *Curriculum Guidance for the Foundation Stage*. London: QCA

Introduction

Although assessment information can be used for many purposes, the most important purpose for us as teachers and TAs is its use to help pupils learn and make progress. In this chapter we will consider assessment issues in the context of the supporting, teaching and learning of literacy and English. Learning and progress in English and literacy in the primary school are vital to pupils' future success. Using assessment effectively can be a powerful tool for motivating pupils and ensuring they receive the appropriate teaching experiences. The statutory basis, underlying ideas and principles relating to supporting processes of assessment have been discussed in chapter 8 of *Becoming a Primary Higher Level Teaching Assistant* (Rose 2005). It would be helpful for you to re-read this chapter as a reminder of definitions and general issues in assessment.

You will probably be aware of changes in the way teachers assess and use assessment information over the last few years. You may have participated in training to implement formative assessment and peer/self-assessment. Recent research in assessment has focused on the impact of formative assessment or Assessment for Learning (AfL). You will recall from reading chapter 8 of Rose (2005) that formative assessment informs our teaching and allows us to give specific feedback that will help pupils make progress in their learning.

It is likely that your school is developing and changing its approach to assessment at the moment. This may give you the opportunity to be involved in training and professional development. You should ensure that you understand your school's philosophy and approach to assessment by reading the school assessment policy. This may be a policy in its own right, part of the learning and teaching policy, or part of subject policies such as the literacy or English policy.

In this chapter we will consider some of the documentation underpinning assessment in literacy and English. Different types of assessment and how they fit with assessment of literacy and English will be explored. We will examine the challenges of assessing speaking and listening, reading and writing including specific aspects such as spelling and phonics. Your role in gathering assessment information, using it to modify planning and teaching and giving formative feedback to pupils will be considered. In particular, this chapter will focus upon the standards highlighted in the box opposite.

CHAPTER OBJECTIVES

By the end of this chapter you should:

● have investigated the relevant documentation available

● have consolidated your understanding of assessment strategies and considered them in relation to literacy and English

● have considered issues related to assessment in literacy and English in particular

● have explored effective formative feedback to pupils and teachers in literacy and English.

Documents and supporting information

As you will be aware, there is a great deal of documentation and information arriving at schools. Although you may not need to have all of it to hand all of the time, it is useful for you, as a professional TA, to know what is available and be ready it to consult it where appropriate.

You will know from looking at the National Curriculum Handbook that there are level descriptions for each of the attainment targets. In English there are level descriptions for En1 Speaking and listening, En2 Reading and En3 Writing. For each of these there is a series of level descriptions from Level 1 to Level 8 providing the basis for assessing pupils' performance at the end of each key stage. Teachers use assessment evidence to come to a judgement about which level description best describes the attainment of the pupil. Reading the level descriptions for English attainment targets will give you an overview of expectations. This can be useful when you are planning your support and teaching.

You will have noticed when reading the level descriptions that they start at Level 1 and that each describes a relatively large step in terms of progress. If you support pupils who are working at below Level 1, or whose progress is slower than that of most pupils, there is additional documentation to support teachers and TAs. These differentiated performance criteria are called 'P scales'. The descriptions are available on the QCA website along with guidance on their use. They are becoming more a part of assessment in primary schools now since schools were asked to report on the attainment of pupils who do not achieve Level 1 at the end of Key Stage 1 using P scales.

For pupils who are learning English as an additional language there is specific guidance on assessment in the QCA document *A Language in Common* published in 2000. This provides schools with a common scale to pursue for assessment, with extended scales of assessment. These include two steps before Level 1 and two descriptions for performance at Level 1, threshold and secure, then moving on to National Curriculum Level 2. If you are working with pupils who are learning English as additional language it is likely that there will be teachers and TAs who can give you guidance on this area of assessment. You will find examples of assessment in *A Language in Common* that you may also find useful.

While you are unlikely to be called upon to judge a pupils' National Curriculum level on your own, it will help you in your role if you develop a good working understanding of performance levels. This will enable you to give appropriate feedback to the teacher and and plan learning experiences that support progress.

Types of assessment

You will be aware from reading 'Supporting the processes of assessment' in *Becoming a Primary Higher Level TA* that there are a number of ways we can assess pupils' progress, attainment and achievement.

Formative assessment or assessment for learning

Assessment for learning (AfL) has been defined as 'the process of seeking and interpreting evidence for use by learners and their teachers to decide where the learners are in their learning, where they need to go and how best to get there'.

(Assessment Reform Group, DfES 2002, p.10)

As a professional TA you will often find yourself in the position to give formative feedback to pupils as you support them in their learning and they share their learning outcomes with you. Formative feedback is most effective when it is based specifically on the learning objective and success criteria that underpin the learning activity. General feedback such as 'well done' or 'lovely work' does not give the pupils any understanding of what they have done well and should keep doing and where they need to improve and how to do this. This kind of feedback can also be based on learning targets in Individual Education Plans. Giving effective formative feedback can be challenging for teachers and TAs but can be very motivating for pupils and is a powerful way of maintaining and improving their self-esteem. The ways we give oral and written feedback are areas for consideration. An example of this is supplied in the case study in Chapter 4.

Summative assessment or assessment of learning

Summative assessment provides teachers and TAs with a snapshot of what pupils know, can do and/or understand at a given moment. This information can be used to check a pupils' progress over a period of time, make comparisons to a set of standards or expectations such as level descriptions and allow us to consider the effectiveness of our teaching. The information you gather in summative assessment can be used formatively to make changes to the teaching programme for individuals, groups and the whole class. For example, if you test pupils' acquisition of sight vocabulary you may use the assessment information to identify pupils who need additional support, a different approach or extension activities. You may also give the pupils feedback on their progress since the last check, which can motivate them to persevere.

Normative assessment

Normative assessment involves using tests of ability, achievement or attainment in which the individual pupils' achievements can be compared to a 'standardised sample' of pupils on whom the test was trialled. It can give us a description of the pupils' achievements compared to those of similar age. As a professional TA you may encounter this type of assessment as it can be used to identify pupils who are performing below the level expected for their age. You may then be supporting these pupils through their IEPs, group work and catch-up programmes in and out of the classroom.

Diagnostic assessment

Diagnostic assessment involves a detailed assessment in order to investigate the precise nature of pupils' problems in a specific area. This can be useful where pupils have a specific learning difficulty in an area of the curriculum. As a professional TA you may be using the results of diagnostic assessment to base support programmes on or you may be trained in administering some diagnostic tests. Again the key importance of this assessment information is that we use it to improve learning and progress. In English you might use a miscue analysis in reading to identify areas where additional support is needed and also areas of strength upon which to build.

Ipsative assessment

Ipsative assessment involves us helping individual pupils compare themselves to their own previous best. Clearly it can be a powerful vehicle for acknowledging personal achievement and progress. It can be used to boost self-esteem, improve confidence and motivate pupils towards further success. If it is the policy of your school to keep assessment folders of pupils' previous work on a regular basis, this can be used to base discussions with them about how much they have learned and improved over time and what their targets or learning focus will be in the next half term or term.

Self- and peer assessment

Recent research has also focused on the importance of involving the pupils themselves in self-assessment and peer assessment. Equipping pupils with the skills to evaluate their own learning and identify areas for development contributes towards their independence as learners. 'Teachers should equip learners with the desire and the capacity to take charge of their learning through developing the skills of self-assessment'. (Assessment Reform Group, 2002). Even the very youngest pupils can begin to be involved in self-assessment through using visual prompts such as faces and hand signals. Smiley faces and actions.

Assessing speaking and listening

As Grugeon *et al.* (2001) suggest, it can be particularly challenging to assess pupils' progress in speaking and listening for a number of reasons, including the ephemeral nature of the evidence and the number of pupils in the class. Your role as a professional TA is crucial in this area. In the literacy hour in particular there will be times when you are with the class in whole-class teaching time. This may give you the opportunity to observe speaking and listening while the teacher teaches the lesson.

As a professional TA you will be contributing your observations of pupils' speaking and listening skills on a day-to-day basis using formal strategies and picking up informal details too. Schools organise the way they collect and store assessment information about speaking and listening in many ways. For some groups of pupils' language profiles or surveys may be used to ensure that significant information is collected and available for teachers and TAs to use as the basis of their teaching and planning. Edwards (1995) has provided a useful model for a language survey for pupils learning English as an additional language, and this is worthwhile activity for all pupils.

Giving pupils opportunities to talk about speaking and listening helps them reflect upon how they use, change and extend their learning about speaking and listening. As Grugeon *et al.* (2001) suggest, making our implicit knowledge explicit is an important aspect of developing pupils' speaking and listening. An effective strategy for helping pupils start to self-assess can be to devise and share success criteria clearly and in a child-friendly manner. An example of this is discussed in the case study on page 112.

PRACTICAL TASK

Over the course of a week observe two pupils. You could consult with the class teacher on which pupils to choose. Complete the observation chart.

	PUPIL A	PUPIL B
How often does the pupil volunteer to answer or join in?		
How often is the pupil asked to join in?		
Are the contributions: single words, phrases, a single sentence, or a sustained contribution? (examples)		
Are the contributions well-organised and correctly sequenced?		
Does the pupil use vocabulary appropriate to the subject, the pupils' age? (examples)		
How does the pupil use: expression, animation, tone of voice?		
Other comments		

Discuss your observations with the class teacher. Consider the following the questions:

- What are the strengths of each pupil?

- What are the areas for development for each pupil?

- How do these observations fit with your experience of the pupils across the curriculum?

- Were there any implications for the whole class?

In this case study Zoe is able to involve pupils in understanding what success looks like and how they can practise and take steps towards improvement. Adults can use these clear success criteria to prompt and praise pupils. Pupils get the opportunity to use their speaking and listening skills in a meaningful context that develops their independence and confidence. As she develops this work around the school, Zoe can identify other opportunities and applications of this approach.

Older pupils can discuss and compile their own success criteria at the level appropriate for their learning. An example of this is given on the DfES video *Speaking, Listening, Learning* in the Year 4 term 1 clip. In this some pupils act as observers using the shared criteria to give positive and formative feedback to their friends. The teacher has established a classroom culture to ensure that this type of activity is conducted positively.

Case study

Zoe is a TA who supports around the school, in both Key Stages 1 and 2. She is aware that the school is working on developing the pupils' speaking and listening skills. She also knows that often when younger or less confident pupils are asked to take messages to other classes or the office, sometimes it is a challenge to unravel them! She suggests that each class develop a set of criteria to describe how to take a message. This will allow pupils to be clear about this popular task and all adults to help and praise effectively. These are presented as posters in each classroom and reflect the developing independence as pupils get older.

> When we take a message we:
>
> Listen carefully to the message
>
> Repeat it to check we remember it
>
> Say excuse me if the person is talking or busy
>
> Look at the person we are talking to
>
> Speak loudly and clearly

Assessing reading

Your role in the assessment of reading is vital to both pupils and teachers. Giving formative feedback in relation to individual or lesson objectives is motivating for pupils, as they see that their progress is recognised and valued. Supplying appropriate feedback to teachers and other adults reading with pupils is vital to planning effective reading experiences for the pupil or group over time. The case study in Chapter 4 helped us to consider how a TA can give positive and development feedback when reading with pupils. Working from clearly stated, shared learning objectives or targets underpins this. In Chapter 6 coaching and scaffolding pupils' use of phonics were explored. Again this is a form of formative assessment that you can use when reading with pupils.

It may be that your most frequent involvement in assessment of reading is that of ongoing assessment as the pupil reads. As well as providing positive and development feedback to the pupil another important aspect of your role here is to provide records for the teacher and other adults who read with the pupil. In guided reading you could do this through annotating the plan or using a grid containing the names of each pupil in your group. When reading with individuals you perhaps make notes in the pupils' reading diary. The most important feature of your feedback should be that it is informative and helpful to the next adult who reads with the pupil. It could be related to any reading targets or identified areas for development and indicate how the pupil is progressing towards these, or note errors that you might discuss with the teacher later. A general comment 'read well' and page numbers 'read p. 1 to 8' is less useful.

As a professional TA it is likely your role will involve you in more than day-to-day, ongoing assessment. You may be implementing programmes to support individuals or groups making progress towards their curricular targets over a term or longer. In order to do this you must develop an understanding of the assessment criteria used in your school and how the programmes you are working on can help pupils reach their targets. Using intervention programmes at the appropriate time, effectively and flexibly is a feature of effective schools (Ofsted 2005). Most published and DfES support programmes have support materials that you can read and discuss with the class teacher. Talking with the teacher about how the individual needs of pupils fit within the programme will help you see how far you can adapt to meet the needs of the pupils within the overall prescribed structure or framework.

You may also have been involved in or seen teachers gathering information about pupils' reading through completing a miscue analysis using a running record. This is a useful strategy for having a very close look at the reading of the individual pupil, perhaps of a pupil you are concerned about or just need to know more about the strategies the pupil uses when reading. Teachers who have taught Year 2 and administered Key Stage 1 assessment tasks in reading will be familiar with this process and can guide you. Further support material is available in the DfES document and video *Guided Reading: Supporting Transition from KS 1 to KS 2*, where using a running record and analysing errors to support planning next steps is demonstrated.

Assessing writing

Recent research has shown that when responding to pupils' writing most teachers give feedback to pupils about presentation, surface features, quantity and effort before considering the learning objective for the writing task (Clarke 2001). This tends to shift the pupils' focus to the aspects mentioned by the teacher or TA, often at the expense of the learning objective. Although handwriting, spelling and punctuation are important and comments about them come to mind easily, we must guard against inadvertently conveying to pupils these are always the most important feature to concentrate on. If the learning objective is concerned with use of words and ideas or development of plot and character, these are the aspects of writing that our first and most detailed feedback should be discussed with pupils.

Many schools now use the learning intention and success criteria as a basis for formative assessment in writing. There is an example of this in the case study in Chapter 5. Teachers also use individual writing targets with pupils and again use these to guide their formative assessment and feedback in a focused way. In addition to this, a form of marking called 'closing the gap' marking is a very powerful tool for improving writing through formative feedback. Your use of these strategies should, of course, be guided by your school's assessment policy. You can read more about them in the books of Shirley Clarke (see References).

Summary

Effective assessment in English involves:

- giving formative and development feedback based on learning intentions, success criteria or targets
- having a clear understanding of assessment criteria
- choosing the most appropriate tool for assessment
- using assessment information to help learners and teachers.

References

Assessment Reform Group (2002) *Assessment for Learning: Ten Principles*. London: QCA.

Clarke, S. (1998) *Targeting Assessment in the Primary School*. London: Hodder and Stoughton

Clarke, S. (2001) *Unlocking Formative Assessment*. London: Hodder and Stoughton.

Clarke, S. (2003) *Enriching Feedback in the Primary Classroom*. London: Hodder and Stoughton

Department for Education and Skills (2003) *Guided Reading: Supporting Transition from KS 1 to KS 2*. London: DfES

Edwards, V. (1995) *Speaking and Listening in Multilingual Classrooms*. University of Reading: Reading and Language Information Centre. Department for Education and Skills

Grugeon, E., Hubbard, H., Smith, C. and Dawes, L. (eds) (2001) *Teaching Speaking and Listening in the Primary School*. London: David Fulton

QCA. (2000) *A Language in Common*. London: QCA

Rose, R. (2005) *Becoming a Higher Level Primary Teaching Assistant*. Exeter: Learning Matters

Index

Higher Level Teaching Assistants

These practical guides provide a helpful combination of theory and practice for all teaching assistants on training and assessment routes to Higher Level Teaching Assistant status. The books are cross-referenced to the HLTA standards throughout, and include case studies, practical tasks and references to key theory and research. They emphasise the increasingly professional approach of teaching assistants working in modern classrooms. You can find out more information on each of these titles by visiting our website: www.learningmatters.co.uk

Becoming a Primary Higher Level Teaching Assistant
Richard Rose
160pp ISBN 10: 1 84445 025 2 ISBN 13: 978 1 84445 025 1

Becoming a Higher Level Teaching Assistant: Primary English
Jean Edwards
128pp ISBN 10: 1 84445 046 5 ISBN 13: 978 1 84445 046 6

Becoming a Higher Level Teaching Assistant: Primary Mathematics
Debbie Morgan
112pp ISBN 10: 1 84445 043 0 ISBN 13: 978 1 84445 043 5

Becoming a Higher Level Teaching Assistant: Primary Special Educational Needs
Mary Doveston, Steve Cullingford-Agnew
128pp ISBN 10: 1 84445 052 X ISBN 13: 978 1 84445 052 7